Holding Back The Tide

The Thirty-Five Year Struggle to Save Montauk

A History of the Concerned Citizens of Montauk

Holding Back The Tide

The Thirty-Five Year Struggle to Save Montauk

A History of the Concerned Citizens of Montauk

Joan Powers Porco

Preface by Edward Albee

New York | Sag Harbor
Harbor Electronic Publishing
www.HEPDigital.com
2005

Map of Montauk

New York State Parks, County Preserves, and East Hampton Town Reserved Land

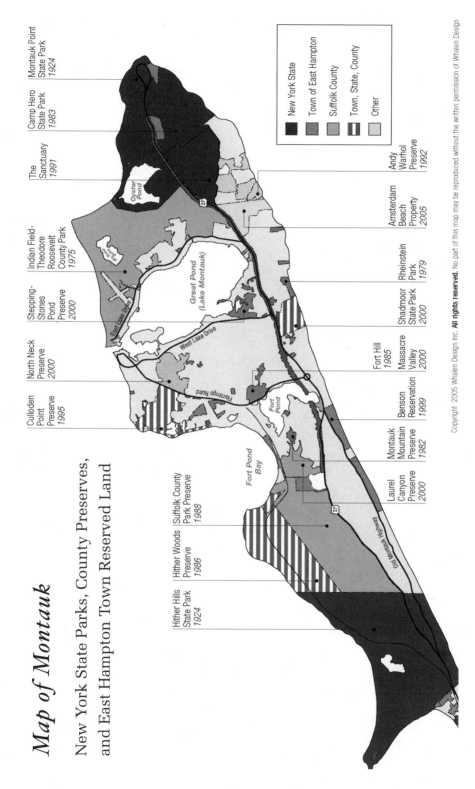

Legend:
- New York State
- Town of East Hampton
- Suffolk County
- Town, State, County
- Other

Hither Hills State Park 1924

Hither Woods Preserve 1986

Suffolk County Park Preserve 1988

Culloden Point Preserve 1995

North Neck Preserve 2000

Stepping-Stones Pond Preserve 2000

Indian Field-Theodore Roosevelt County Park 1975

The Sanctuary 1991

Camp Hero State Park 1983

Montauk Point State Park 1924

Laurel Canyon Preserve 2000

Montauk Mountain Preserve 1982

Benson Reservation 1999

Massacre Valley 2000

Fort Hill 1985

Shadmoor State Park 2000

Rheinstein Park 1979

Amsterdam Beach Property 2005

Andy Warhol Preserve 1992

Fort Pond Bay

Fort Pond

Great Pond (Lake Montauk)

Oyster Pond

Old Montauk Highway

Flamingo Road

West Lake Drive

East Lake Drive

© 2005 by Concerned Citizens of Montauk, Inc.
Library of Congress Control Number: 2005932095
ISBN 10 1-932916-05-9 (paper)
ISBN 13 978-1-932916-05-8 (paper)
ISBN 10 1-932916-06-7 (eBook)

Printed in the United States of America.
First printing: October 2005.

This print version of the book does not include an index. Readers who need an index are directed to the eBook version, which is fully word-searchable.

Edited by Anne Sanow
Design by Charles Monaco
Cover design by Joseph Dunn
Photos by Bill Akin, Céline Keating, Peter Lowenstein, Larry Smith, and other CCOM Directors
Cover photo by Walter Iooss, Jr.

Dedication

This book is dedicated to the CCOM members and directors—living and deceased—who over the years have spent thousands of hours attending town meetings, sending out mailings, creating, printing, and putting up posters, writing letters, donating money, offering free legal assistance, urging neighbors into action, organizing events, raising money, making movies, writing newsletters, keeping the books, travelling to Albany and Washington, and protesting from Montauk to Manhattan: those who walk the walk, those who back up their words with deeds.

You know who you are.

"Like so many other old parts of America, this basically agricultural area is now deeply, perhaps suicidally, threatened by massive development. Zoning fights, battles over land use, pollution problems, real estate speculators, nature lovers, village merchants, frantic tourists, greed, stupidity and vested interests threaten to tear the place apart.... If these last fields and villages are allowed to go the way the rest of Long Island has gone—raped, cut up, paved over and left to die piecemeal—there will be nowhere left to go. This is literally the last place."

—Shana Alexander, *Newsweek*, August 7, 1972

"In the end, our society will be defined not by what it creates, but by what it refuses to destroy."

—John Sawhill (1936–2000)

Table of Contents

A note to readers:

This book was compiled primarily from numerous interviews with CCOM Board members, past and present, as well with other members of the East Hampton and Montauk communities. While the author and editors have made efforts to confirm certain historical facts, most of what is contained reflects how individuals remember the events that are discussed. Others who were involved will no doubt recall events differently.

Also, while CCOM was involved to a greater or lesser extent in all the events discussed, this history is by no means intended to minimize the efforts of other groups and individuals who were involved and contributed in many ways.

Finally, on place names in Long Island's East End: Montauk—along with Amagansett and Napeague—are hamlets, rather than individual villages or towns. All three fall under the official jurisdiction of East Hampton Town. Thus, throughout the book, readers should understand that when "Town" is capitalized, it refers to East Hampton Town.

Preface

AVE YOU EVER WANTED TO READ A BOOK where the good people win and the bad people are defeated?

"Sure!" you say. "I love reading fiction!"

Well, what you're looking at right now is a book where the good people win and the bad people are defeated—but it isn't fiction; it's fact.

It is the story of how a group of citizens who love their town—its beauty, its purity, its simplicity—have done battle for the past 35 years with greedy land speculators, corrupt politicians, and incompetent officials and won!

It is the story of how ordinary citizens educated themselves to the point where they understood all the devious ways those out to rape their town were proceeding, and how to defeat them at their game.

This is the story of The Concerned Citizens of Montauk and the continuing battle, with the names of all the good people and the names of all the bad people right there for you to read.

It is an important story—not only for those of us who live in Montauk and love it (42 years for me!) but a true "how to" book for all citizens who wish to protect their environments from the forces of darkness (sometimes called "progress").

Read it; be proud; learn!

Edward Albee
Montauk, August 2005

Acknowledgements

THE DAY AFTER I COMPLETED THE LAST CHAPTER of this book, my husband Ed and I took one of our favorite hikes into Big Reed Pond, a trail in Theodore Roosevelt County Park. It was a brilliant, sunny July day. Probably because of that, most people were at the beach, we deduced, as we encountered no one on our two-hour walk.

In that silence of the woods and the loveliness of the sunlight-dappled forest, I could not help but think of Hilda Lindley in gratitude for the gift I was experiencing at that very moment. Her gift, and the gift of the concerned and determined band of citizens who have cheerfully been along for the lengthy ride through the quagmires of environmental struggles, is truly a gift that keeps on giving. I could never possibly name them all.

Many have helped and supported me in sorting out the numerous critical events and decisions throughout the decades that have so profoundly impacted on this unique hamlet, Montauk. To be given this opportunity to learn the work of CCOM and present it in some organized form has made me indebted to Bill Akin, president of CCOM, who conceived of the project, and helped keep it on track even when the complexity of the project appeared overwhelming. Vice-President

Céline Keating undertook the unenviable work of editing the manuscript in its raw stages. She did it with superior professionalism but also with respect for my efforts and encouragement despite my limitations. What more could anyone want in an editor!

There were many rewarding experiences for me in the two-year process of my work. None more so than my interviews with some of the CCOM founders: in particular Lillian and Dorothy Disken, Kay Carley, Kay Dayton, the feisty Richard Johnson, the undaunted Rita McKernan, and the inimitable Carol Morrison. They were tremendously helpful in providing me with some of the missing archival material that was scattered in shopping bags, garages, attics, as well as in files. I consider them my friends.

Speaking to the many interviewees, who were generous in giving their time to help weave the threads of CCOM's story from their own experiences, was a testament to their valuation of the organization. I thank them all. One of the most unforgettable and moving of those interviews was offered by John Lindley, who graciously consented to an interview while Julie Evans-Brumm videotaped us at the Lindley home in the parkland his mother had rescued from the threat of development. It was a truly unique experience that touched me deeply.

Jeanne Nielsen and Eugene De Pasquale of the Tax Assessor's office were most helpful in ferreting out some ancient deeds and archivist Robin Strong, at the Montauk Library, could not have been more helpful. Jodi Grindrod helped where she could, as did Julie Evans-Brumm.

David Rattray and Alice Ragusa at the *East Hampton Star* proved invaluable. David cooperated wholeheartedly by making the *Star*'s archives available and Alice combed through decades of articles and photographs more than once turning up events I had never heard mentioned in my interviews.

The collection of aerial photos could never have been possible without Peter Lowenstein. On two occasions he piloted his plane while others used his camera to record the landscape below.

Before it was final, the manuscript needed to be reviewed and revised for accuracy. To this end I called on Rav Freidel, Richard Kahn, Russell Stein, and Carol Morrison. Everyone made valuable and extensive contributions.

Publisher James Monaco saw the importance of telling the story of a grassroots group like ours, and with encouragement, support—and gentle nudging—helped bring the book to fruition. Editor Anne Sanow provided needed streamlining and an eye to what outsiders would need to know to appreciate the history. Charles Monaco and Joe Dunn, respectively, provided the alchemy that turned the manuscript into a book with their excellent production and art direction skills.

Not to be ignored by any means, is my husband, Edward Porco, who gallantly and uncomplainingly rescued me countless times when my lap top computer was misbehaving. And my son, Matthew Chachere, was the patient fail-safe backup for a mother who all too often was technologically challenged.

This has truly been an exciting journey.

Joan Powers Porco
July 2005

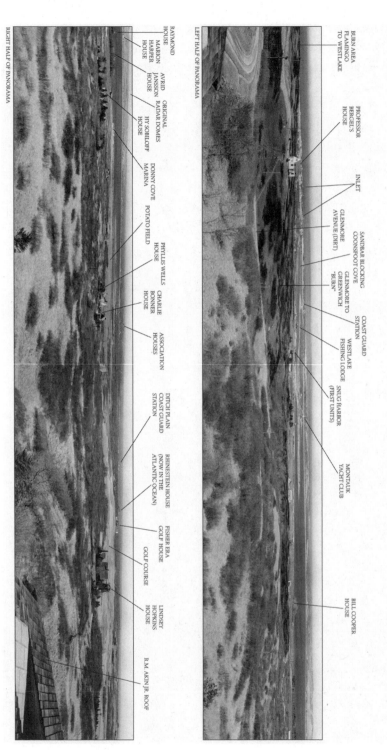

MONTAUK 1957

~ LEGEND ~

LEFT HALF OF PANORAMA

- BURN AREA FLAMINGO TO WESTLAKE
- PROFESSOR BERGEL'S HOUSE
- INLET
- SANDBAR BLOCKING COONSFOOT COVE
- GLENMORE AVENUE (DIRT)
- GLENMORE TO GREENWICH "BURN"
- COAST GUARD STATION
- WESTLAKE FISHING LODGE
- SNUG HARBOR (FIRST UNITS)
- MONTAUK YACHT CLUB
- BILL COOPER HOUSE

RIGHT HALF OF PANORAMA

- RAYMOND HOUSE
- MARION HARPER HOUSE
- AVRID JANSSON HOUSE
- ORIGINAL RADAR DOMES
- HY SOBILOFF HOUSE
- DONNY COVE MARINA
- POTATO FIELD
- PHYLLIS WELLS HOUSE
- CHARLIE BONNER HOUSE
- ASSOCIATION HOUSES
- DITCH PLAIN COAST GUARD STATION
- RHINESTEIN HOUSE (NOW IN THE ATLANTIC OCEAN)
- FISHER ERA GOLF HOUSE
- GOLF COURSE
- LINDSEY HOPKINS HOUSE
- R.M. AKIN JR. ROOF

Introduction

The Montauk Story

L ONG ISLAND STRETCHES FROM THE NEW YORK CITY boroughs of Brooklyn and Queens to a lonely, wind-blown point 120 miles east in the Atlantic Ocean. Montauk is the name the Indians gave to this last place, and if one had never driven the length of Long Island, it would be hard to imagine that these final 12 miles could be part of the same country—much less the same state.

Acres of forest parkland extend from Block Island Sound across the two-mile peninsula, until steep eroded bluffs fall off into the ocean. Looking west from the centuries-old Montauk lighthouse, a rocky coast gives way to small shifting beaches and then finally to long stretches of uninterrupted sand and dunes. Hidden in the interior are dozens of small lakes and ponds that are home to a variety of fish, waterfowl, and wildlife. All of this is surrounded by the rich ocean waters that attracted the first early sportsmen to Montauk.

It seems that everyone who visits this lonely peninsula falls in love with it. The first to make their home here were the American Indians, who thrived on fish and wild game. In the 18th century they shared the land with the East Hampton proprietors, who grazed their cattle every summer on the bountiful prairie grass. These proprietors forced the Indians off the peninsula in the 19th century. The few who remained left when Arthur Benson bought their land in 1879 for a hunting and fishing preserve for the pleasure of his friends. He engaged Frederick Olmstead and Stanford White to design a colony. The military, when it returned from the Spanish American War in the Caribbean, was quarantined in Indian Field, at what is today Theodore Roosevelt County Park.

Sharing Montauk today is a year-round population of less than 4,000 local people. This number leaps to more than 22,000 summer residents made up of tourists, second-home owners, yachtsmen, and home renters.

Critical to understanding how Montauk came to embody such an unlikely contrast of resort destination, working community, and nature sanctuary is the story of one volunteer organization, the Concerned Citizens of Montauk, the members of which have fought since 1970 to save this unique place from becoming another victim of unbridled development.

But the seeds of conflict between those who saw something special in Montauk to protect, and those who saw mostly profit in the ocean views and sandy beaches, began in the early part of the twentieth century. It was 1924 when two larger-than-life men confronted each other over what was then 10,000 acres of cattle pasture. First came Robert Moses, the brash head of the newly created Long Island Parks Commission, announcing his intention to establish 24 parks—starting with two in Montauk. At that time Montauk was owned by the estate of the late Arthur Benson.

What started as a friendly negotiation between Moses and the Benson estate suddenly turned hostile when Miami Beach real estate tycoon, Carl Fisher, began talking about his plans to develop Montauk as a northern counterpart to his just-completed Miami success story. The Bensons immediately jacked their price up from less than $50 an acre to $250. Undeterred, in August of 1924 Moses seized land for his parks using New York State's right of eminent domain: 158 acres near the Montauk lighthouse, and 1,700 acres in the area now known as Hither Hills State Park.

One year later, Carl Fisher bought the remaining 9,000 acres of Montauk for $2.5 million and set about to execute his grand scheme. By 1927 he had completed work on several impressive buildings: the huge Tudor-style Montauk Manor hotel, a seven-story office tower, the Montauk Yacht Club, an 18-hole golf course, polo fields, and a flamingo pink art deco beach club, complete with an Olympic-sized saltwater swimming pool. Unencumbered by any worries about the environment, he also bulldozed a hole in the dunes between Block Island Sound and what was then the largest freshwater lake on Long Island— Lake Montauk—to create a safe harbor for yachts and fishing boats.

Less noticeable, but equally influential on Montauk's future, Fisher filed 10 maps laying out a plan for where and how residential development would proceed. With no regard for Montauk's unique hill-and-dale topography, limited water supply, or drainage patterns, Fisher's plan resulted in a patchwork of half-acre and smaller lots. The sole purpose of this subdivision was to maximize financial gain.

Slow real estate sales in Miami Beach in 1927 and 1928 stretched Fisher's finances and slowed progress on his Montauk development. Then in 1929, the stock market crash cut the foundation out from under the roaring twenties building boom—taking Carl Fisher with it. On May 26, 1932, the Montauk Beach Development Corporation and its primary stockholder, Carl Graham Fisher, declared bankruptcy at the other end of Long Island in a Brooklyn court.

In the years up to and including World War II and continuing through most of the 1950s, development in Montauk was almost nonexistent, with the exception of a military contingent who served at Camp Hero near the lighthouse, and who stayed to make Montauk their home. In the absence of any interest from out-of-town buyers, a small number of local families began to acquire significant holdings of Montauk real estate from what had been Fisher's Montauk empire, as managed by various bank holding companies. Montauk was also growing as a commercial fishing center, which brought fishermen from as far away as Nova Scotia. During the 1950s Montauk's reputation as a prime sportfishing location started to attract a few adventuresome "summer people." To these outsiders, prices still seemed more than reasonable. In 1956, after a few scotches at the already well-known

Shagwong Tavern, one proud new owner was caught boasting how he had just bought an estate with three houses and 25 acres of hilltop property for just over $50,000. A friend and local realtor told him that he thought it was a lousy deal, he was busy buying ocean-front property at one dollar a foot.

As the Long Island road system improved—including the infamous Long Island Expressway—the building boom began. Land prices started to accelerate in the 1960s, and local residents who had suffered through 30 years of hard times began to recognize the potential of Montauk real estate as a means to supplement whatever income they were making from commercial fishing and the limited tourist trade.

In 1970, one proposed development that embodied all the short-sighted aspects of Fisher planning, as well as the new land rush mentality, collided with the new phenomenon of environmental activism. This happened to coincide with the year of the first national Earth Day. The result was the formation of the Concerned Citizens of Montauk, an organization that has ever since fought to preserve Montauk's unique wilderness and to guard the purity of its bays, harbors, lakes, and freshwater supply. Today approximately 60% of the Montauk peninsula is preserved open space. How this was accomplished was not an easy endeavor—CCOM volunteers frequently attended two and even three meetings a day on different problems, waiting three and four hours to make sure public officials heard what they had to say. And the group was not popular with many in the Montauk community. In 1997, a 100-year history of Montauk included a list of every community organization—no matter how small or how new—with the exception of CCOM. And it was CCOM that had worked more than anybody to preserve what was being written about. This is the story of this organization and the people who volunteered because they loved Montauk.

Bill Akin
Summer 2005

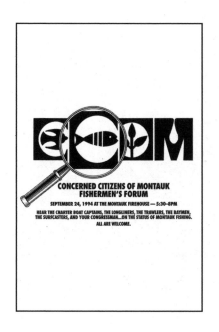

CONCERNED CITIZENS OF MONTAUK
FISHERMEN'S FORUM

SEPTEMBER 24, 1994 AT THE MONTAUK FIREHOUSE — 5:30–8PM

HEAR THE CHARTER BOAT CAPTAINS, THE LONGLINERS, THE TRAWLERS, THE BAYMEN,
THE SURFCASTERS, AND YOUR CONGRESSMAN...ON THE STATUS OF MONTAUK FISHING.
ALL ARE WELCOME.

Chapter 1

Seeds of an

Organization

E ACH SPRING MILLIONS OF ALEWIFE—most would call them minnows—spawn in the Little Reed Pond estuary. They are a crucial part of the local aquatic food chain, and their only route
into Lake Montauk and beyond runs through a single pipe under East
Lake Drive. That's the good news. Because in 1970, the chairman of the
East Hampton Zoning Board of Appeals, Eugene D. Haas Jr., proposed
damming Lake Montauk just south of the Yacht Club and then cutting a
new inlet through Little Reed Pond out to Block Island Sound by Shagwong Point. He also wanted to build 1,400 houses on the 1,000-acre
historic home and burial ground of the Montaukett Indians—known as
Indian Field[1]—adjacent to Big Reed Pond. That would have been very
bad news for the alewife—as well as the Montauk community.

MONTAUKERS FORM GROUP, declared the headline in the July 16,
1970 *East Hampton Star*. "A new committee calling itself Concerned
Citizens of Montauk was formed last week to oppose a recent proposal

---

1. The terms Indian Field and Indian Fields have been used inter-
changeably in documents.

Little Reed Pond is a critical finfish nursery, but it was almost replaced by a new inlet to Lake Montauk in 1970.

for the development of the Indian Field–Lake Montauk area." The article went on to state that the committee included Mrs. Samuel H. Joyce Jr., president of the Montauk Historical Society, and that it had placed an ad in the newspaper opposing the development of Indian Field. It quoted what would become a far-sighted warning by Hilda Lindley, the initiator of the group and owner of a home in Indian Field: "Mass development poses a real threat to the available water supply, in addition to destroying some of the area's most precious natural resources." From this small beginning, the advent of the movement to preserve Montauk's open space and unspoiled water was heralded.

In 1970 Montauk was a community of 3,000 year-round residents, swelling to 18,000 in the summer. Most of the peninsula was still open space: forests and harbors, and a good deal of unspoiled land. The idea of developing Montauk as a resort wasn't a new one. Some in the business community at that time thought that the additional homes would bolster the economy and increase the tax rolls.

The last two miles of Long Island is covered with parkland. Theodore Roosevelt County Park in the foreground; Montauk Point State Park on the left; Camp Hero State Park upper left.

The Indian Field development proposal became a call to action for Hilda Lindley. A remarkable, energetic single mother of three who had been summering in Montauk with her family for many years, she considered Haas's plan an environmental assault. Having seen and been appalled by the destruction of the dunes by developers at nearby Culloden Shores, with its Leisurama cookie-cutter houses, she saw that this concept could easily produce a similar result.[2]

Lindley's home in Indian Field was a former World War II submarine spotting station disguised to look like a farmhouse, with cement clapboard, which she purchased in 1951 as Army surplus. It was located on a high hill near an Army radar station. "It had a clapboard finish they did with cement. The house still had the little holes for the

2. One resident recalls that in preparation for the building of the subdivision in the Culloden Shores area, bulldozers had decimated it so that "it looked like the Gobi Desert."

The house of CCOM founder Hilda Lindley sits alone in the center of Theodore Roosevelt County Park. If CCOM had failed in its first cause this house would have had 1,400 neighbors.

guns.... She [Hilda] was an editor and she was here every weekend and had someone to stay with [the children] during the week, so the children stayed the summer," recalled Carol Morrison, who was a good friend of Lindley's. (Morrison, an economist, had purchased her Hither Hills home in 1967.) According to Hilda's son John, Hilda considered her humble little house "the real home for my family."

First Steps

Within days after the July publication of the Haas plan, Hilda Lindley took action. She called upon her closest neighbors on East Lake Drive, Helen Winberg and Mildred Shapiro, to discuss her concerns about the outcome of the plan. The women met around a handsome wooden table built by another neighbor, Sam Joyce, to consider their options. The women named themselves the Concerned Citizens of Montauk, and decided to run an ad in the *East Hampton Star*. "We really didn't have a plan at that point," Lindley was later quoted as saying in a *New York Times* story of July 1971. "We felt that we might get some support

The house of CCOM founder Hilda Lindley was built in WW II to look like a summer cottage, but the concrete walls are two feet thick and the windows more suitable for gun sites than viewing the sunset.

because the housing plan could endanger Montauk's fresh water supply—we rely entirely on well water."

DO YOU LOVE MONTAUK? that first ad asked. It asked those who thought that Indian Field should be saved to send their name, address, and five dollars.

"We were just overwhelmed by the replies to the ad," the *Times* article quoted Mildred Shapiro, who was to become publicity chair for the group. "We got 80 letters and $400, enough to pay for the ad." Helen Winberg added, "Equally important, we found out that there were more than three of us who wanted to save Indian Field. That was tremendously heartening."

Encouraged by that response, the women, along with restaurant owner John Gosman and Theodore Monell, an executive for the International Nickel Company, called for a public meeting in August. More than 100 people turned out for the meeting. They included some of Lindley's neighbors who lived on East Lake Drive: William Burke, John and Rita Gosman, Tom and Kay Carley, and William and Rita McKernan.

Hilda's House looking west: CCOM founder Hilda Lindley lived in this WW II "bunker house" now in the center of Theodore Roosevelt County Park. Note houses bordering park.

"People either responded to the notice or by word of mouth," recalls Rita McKernan, who became membership chair of CCOM. Her daughter Rita Gosman, and her husband John, a well-known Montauk restaurateur and fish wholesaler, became active as well.

One of the letters responding to the initial ad was signed by sisters Dorothy and Lillian Disken, both schoolteachers in Brooklyn and Queens. They had bought their home in 1963. Dorothy described that next CCOM meeting. "There were about 100 people who met behind the Historical Society, and we were swatting mosquitos. [Later] Hilda said to me, 'Dorothy, you'll be treasurer.' I said I can't manage my own checkbook. She said, 'you'll be fine.' That's how officers were selected." Tom Carley became Vice President, Kay Dayton was named Recording Secretary, and Helen Winburg was designated Corresponding Secretary. John Gosman became a board member, as did Carol Morrison, Helen Sarvis, and James Proctor, among others.

"Hilda was an impressive woman. She knew her own mind and gathered many people together to defend the beautiful area she lived in," Rita McKernan asserts. Kay Dayton confirms this impression: "Hilda was a very beautiful, interesting woman. She was quite dynamic—you could tell the minute you got involved with her."

Carol Morrison remembers that "Nothing daunted her. To give an example, we used to drive back and forth to New York City Friday night and go back Sunday. One Friday it was pouring rain. We got to Montauk and I said, 'Hilda, you don't want to go up the hill to your house. Come to my house and I'll take you first thing in the morning.' Uh-uh. She wouldn't hear of it. She wanted to go up in the pouring rain. I let her off on the dirt road in high heels and city clothes. It was a mile walk—a good healthy walk. But when she made up her mind about something, she made up her mind."

At the first official meeting on September 6, 1970, a letter was formulated and presented for the attendees to sign. It was addressed to New York State Assemblyman and Montauk resident Perry Duryea,[3] and stated the group's opposition to the development plan. There were 330 signatures attached.

Efforts Toward Growth

Within the year, Kay Carley was commended for her efforts in helping to develop a membership of 350 people. Membership continued to grow every year. Carley recalls how this was accomplished: "Hilda was outspoken…. When Hilda spoke, everybody listened…. She went to Town Board meetings to show we were a force…. We'd go to all the neighbors' houses. She'd come back waving a check." CCOM also began to hold monthly public meetings on environmental topics.

A confirmed believer in political action, in that first year Lindley inspired the group to inaugurate a drive for registering summer people to vote in Montauk. "Would you like your vote to count?" asked the letter sent out to potential voters. Zoning fights, battles over land use,

---

3. Duryea is often called one of the most powerful Republicans in the state, having served as Assembly speaker for a lengthy period.

pollution problems, real estate speculations, vested interests, and politicians with hidden agendas would all become hot topics for discussion in the years ahead. The summer population would soon become a significant voting block.

"It was a turning point—the smartest thing they ever did because it didn't take that many votes to turn it around," said John Lindley.

Local voting registration is still an important issue. As CCOM President Bill Akin wrote in his newsletter column titled "Second Home, First Love" in June 2002: "... second homeowners, while representing the majority of property ownership and the majority of town revenue as measured by tax dollars, are the least represented by town government. The reason is simple, most second homeowners don't vote here." He goes on to say that "If you are discouraged by seemingly mindless behavior on the part of politicians, register to vote in this town. Local elections are often won or lost by extremely close margins."

There would, however, be a backlash from the effort to enlist second-home owners. According to environmentalist and longtime East Hampton Town Natural Resources Director Larry Penny, "I think they [the locals] felt that CCOM was mainly a bunch of people from the city; they didn't make their living out here.... [they were] kind of elitist." That perception would be one that had many lasting implications for the organization.

Rita McKernan reflects, "They said that we were a bunch of Democrats. That just wasn't true; we were environmentalists. People wouldn't talk to us. They said, 'You people come here and want to change things—why don't you go back where you came from.'"

CCOM did very grassroots organizing in these beginning days. "We went house to house... and took our chances on who would be with us and who wouldn't," Kay Dayton recalls. "Every year we'd study the new tax rolls to see any new owners and write to them and send literature. It just grew and grew, and every year we had a party. People came to that and brought a new person." Dayton noted that it was the later arrivals to the area who became the backbone of the group—they had seen how the rest of Long Island had deteriorated because of overdevelopment. Says Russell Stein:

Why did I join? I went to a couple of Montauk Village Association meetings because I was so unhappy with what I was seeing in Montauk... lots of construction going on... a lot of things for sale. Compared to now it was nothing... it looked like Montauk was going to be ruined. I remember trying to bring that up at the MVA [Montauk Village Association] and nobody was impressed with it.

The Battle for Indian Field Joined

The minutes record that after receiving the letter of opposition, Perry Duryea attended CCOM's October 1970 meeting. He said that a Lake Montauk dam was unfeasible, that in any case the lake bottom belonged to East Hampton Town, and also that there was no serious pollution. Moreover, he claimed, neither state, local, nor county government could provide the $40–50 million needed to buy Indian Field. He suggested working through the state for development of historical sites which could lead to the acquisition of Indian Field in the name of the Town.

But Lindley wasn't about to give up. States John Lindley, "My mother was a person who was very tenacious and who never thought anything was impossible." Kay Carley evidently agrees with his assessment and tears up as she describes Hilda Lindley. "She [Hilda] was a real fighter... I was backing her because I agreed with her. Here she's up there all alone—you had to admire her."

Though the members of the nascent organization were taken with the stunning beauty of the 1,100 acres of former grazing land that was Indian Field, it was obvious that the magnificence of the area wasn't going to be enough to persuade the county to purchase it. Something concrete was needed to help buttress the argument against development. Hilda Lindley found that something thanks to the newly formed Group for America's South Fork, founded in 1972. She immediately became an active board member in the later-renamed Group for the South Fork.

That something was groundwater. "The Group for the South Fork started as a research organization and was giving us material for what we wanted to prove—that the land was worth saving," according to Carol Morrison. "She [Lindley] knew that water was scarce there, and to put 1,400 houses—she just couldn't figure out how that could work. The theme of water [as an issue for CCOM] started from there."

Although Lindley appealed to the federal government as well as the state government to purchase Indian Field, it was from the county and County Executive John V. Klein that she eventually got a sympathetic ear. The county finally approved the purchase of Indian Field on July 18, 1972, having first postponed the purchase until the airport and a "fillet" strip of 40 acres was carved out to remain as private property owned by Perry Duryea.[4]

But first there was also a battle over Hilda Lindley's right to remain in her house on that land. That story made the headlines in the *New York Times* on November 12, 1972. It read: WOMAN'S SUCCESS IN DRIVE FOR L. I. PARK MAY LEAD TO HER EVICTION.

CCOM's newsletter (instituted by the board from the very inception of the group) told the dramatic story of the machinations that had been going on in its January 1973 edition:

> For several weeks prior to the end of the year [1972], the executive board of Concerned Citizens... was engaged in supporting the efforts of our president, Hilda Lindley, to maintain her home in Indian Field, as she was assured a year ago by Suffolk County Park Commissioner Charles Dominy. Although this assurance was backed up by an offer from County Attorney George Percy, on November 1, 1972, of 35-year occupancy for Mrs. Lindley and her children if she would donate the property to the county and pay maintenance, insurance and taxes, on November 3 the four-man

---

4. Remarkably, Klein delayed the taking of the title until an appraisal survey had been completed, since he believed that rising land values placed a higher price than the $4,000,000 that the county had allocated for the purchase of Indian Field. The CCOM newsletter of January 1973 states that "It is obviously more sensible to get an appraisal before voting money for an expensive parcel. CCOM hopes that as the result of the publicity surrounding the Indian Field purchase, the county will institute a new policy for parkland acquisition that will be fair to and understood by both the public and county officials."

Four members of CCOM's original Board of Directors—Rita McKernan, Dorothy Disken, Kaye Carley, and Lillian Disken (left to right)—are honored for 30 years of service (2000).

Suffolk County Park Committee, headed by Thomas Strong, voted unanimously to evict her.

On November 14, twenty-four members of CCOM—many of them taking time off from their jobs—journeyed to Hauppauge, the county center, to urge the 18-member Suffolk County Legislature to allow Lindley to stay in her home. Dorothy Disken recalls, "We took the day off to go; so did others.... We were there to show that others cared about the issue. They tried to imply she had ulterior motives."

"Following that meeting," the CCOM article continued, "Strong met with Lindley and her attorney [Saul Wolf of East Hampton], and offered to work out an agreement by Friday, November 17, but on November 16, he, his committee [and Commissioner Dominy] again voted unanimously to evict her."

On November 28, County Executive Klein asked the legislators to again meet with Lindley to try to work out a compromise. A stormy session followed in Riverhead on December 7, with an intransigent John Strong insisting that Lindley be evicted despite the fact that other families were allowed to stay in their homes on other lands that were purchased to become county parklands.

It was revealed at that meeting that the Parks Committee had adopted a new eviction policy in January of 1972, but had not informed the Parks Commissioner, the County Executive and his deputy, the Legislature, and the county. Everyone but the Parks Committee was unaware of the new policy—and the committee admitted that Lindley was the first to have the new policy applied to her.

INDIAN FIELD: WHY NOT 1,400 HOUSES?

The 1,157 acres that is now Theodore Roosevelt County Park is not only one of the most scenic places on the entire East Coast of the United States, but it is also one of the most ecologically diverse. The 53-acre Big Reed Pond alone is designated by the U.S. Department of the Interior as a National Scenic Landmark. The broad-leaf cattail marsh at the western boarder of the pond is considered the best example of this type of community on Long Island. The National Heritage Program has identified several rare wetland plant species, wild flowers, and dependent wildlife that thrive in the Big Reed ecosystem.

At other locations in the park visitors will find a pristine, and extremely fragile, dune community that contains several flora and fauna species unique to this type of environment. One of the last remaining meadows of maritime grasslands spreads across the open hills, and along with the forest of hickory, beech, red oak, and scarlet oak it is home to red tail fox, white tail deer, rabbit and at least 85 species of breeding birds.

Annually the park is a temporary resting place for dozens of migrating birds, while the beaches provide some of the best striped bass surf-casting between Cape Cod and Cape Hatteras. The Little Reed Pond estuary is the prime breeding ground for tiny alewife minnows that migrate through a pipe under East Lake Drive and become the foundation of the food stock for dozens of local commercial and game fish for which Montauk is famous.

And to think, all this could have been 1,400 home sites.

"It was revenge," Dorothy Disken stated unequivocally.

The editorial page of the November 30, 1972 issue of the *East Hampton Star* conjectured:

> It would appear that someone on the county level simply decided
> to teach Mrs. Lindley a lesson, a lesson perhaps intended for the
> edification of others who might feel like asking probing questions.
> To the argument that private homes don't belong within parks, one
> can point to the Fire Island and Cape Cod National Seashores,
> where long-term tenancy provisions were easily worked out
> between the government and isolated homeowners, and the Cedar
> Point County Park, where the failure to work out such an arrange-
> ment has resulted in the utter vandalizing of Cedar Island Light, a
> historic landmark. This, no doubt, is what will happen to Mrs.
> Lindley's house at Montauk, unless it is transformed into a hunt-
> ing lodge for county bigwigs.

Some suspected that the basis for the "revenge" was Hilda's being an outspoken political partisan. Says Carol Morrison, "Hilda was a Democrat and [she] felt that politics was very, very important." CCOM's reputation was that it was identified with the Democratic Party because Perry Duryea, the Republican leader of the State Assembly, was against the acquisition of Indian Field.

She continues, "That's why many people wouldn't admit they were a member of CCOM. 'You shouldn't do that because Duryea wouldn't like it.' That's where [CCOM] got its partisan reputation. Even though at that time we had a guy like Neal Mahoney, a great guy and a Republican committee person. Tom Carley [who would succeed Lindley to the presidency] was a Republican; Dick Johnson was a Republican. We had Republicans on the board, but that didn't make any difference."

There were other views about Lindley as well. As the organization she'd founded gained momentum, her motivation was called into question. This fact is still painful for John Lindley to remember. Dorothy Disken recalls that during the battle to save her home, some people would say "'Who does she think she is?' or 'She just wants a private park.'"

In an article by Jack Graves in the November 15, 1972 issue of the

Woman's Success in Drive for L.I. Park May Lead to Her Eviction

By DAVID A. ANDELMAN
Special to The New York Times

MONTAUK, L.I., Nov. 12—For nearly five years Hilda Lindley led the fight for a 900-acre county park overlooking Block Island Sound here. Now that fight has been won and the park created, but for Mrs. Lindley the success of the fight may mean eviction from the home she has occupied for 22 years on two acres of land right in the middle of the park site.

Her home is the old Montauk blockhouse, built during World War II as a submarine spotting station on a knoll in the center of what will become Montauk Park.

Although Mrs. Lindley offered last month to give her cottage and two acres of land to the county without charge, in return for permission to continue living on it for 35 years, the County Legislature parks committee rejected her offer last week and voted instead to acquire it at a cost of up to $100,000. The County Legislature is to act on the matter on Tues-day, and Mrs. Lindley may lose her property then unless her friends and attorneys can persuade the county not to take the step.

She and the Concerned Citizens of Montauk, one of Long Island's leading environmental organizations, which Mrs. Lindley founded, still intend, however, to fight for her house despite their having won the battle for the park and the land-bank concept.

Mrs. Hilda Lindley outside her home at Montauk Point, L.I. The area is to become a 900-acre county park.

The New York Times/Robert Walker

"Mrs. Hilda Lindley outside her home at Montauk Point, L.I. The area is to become a 900-acre county park." —*New York Times*, 11/13/1972.

East Hampton Star, at a very disappointing time in the proceedings a "despondent" Hilda Lindley is quoted as saying,

> I feel I am being victimized; the surrounding private properties will increase in value. Those owners are being greatly enriched [by having a county park adjacent to their properties], while I'm being deprived of my home and land through condemnation, which carries a price much lower than market value. I will have to sell at a loss and lose occupancy; it's a cruel reward for one who's worked so hard to preserve this land.
>
> A lot of people say I'm being stupid, that I should take the money, but the things I care about are things money can't buy. If I had it to do all over again, knowing that it would end this way, I still would have done it. People need this land; it will be a place they can go to recover from their tensions. It will be a much better tourist attraction for Montauk than motels.

Mary Ella Reutershan of Amagansett, who would later become an East Hampton Town councilwoman, appeared on Lindley's behalf before the County Legislature on November 28. Two days later the *Star* reported that she asked the following:

- For an explanation of "the strange shape of the taking area [of the Indian Field park] and the apparently careful exclusion of certain rather valuable properties."
- Why the Proximar development in which she said State Assembly Speaker Perry B. Duryea, Jr. was "allegedly" a partner, had been deleted from the taking area.
- Whether "the county in fact plans an expansion of the Montauk airstrip and the full-scale development of a county airport," using 43 acres surrounding the airstrip that it had acquired for "county purposes, not for the park." Mr. Duryea was a founder of the airstrip.
- How the Legislators had arrived at the purchase figure of the park land, $4,035,000.

On December 12, 1972 the Legislators finally voted 14 to 0 to authorize the County Attorney to negotiate an occupancy agreement with Lindley based on her initial proposal that if the county would buy the land, she would give her house to the new park when she died. The *New York Times* quoted Lindley as saying: "The best I can hope for is some arrangement for lifetime use. I shouldn't mind, because the important thing is that an area I love is going to be kept untouched. My own inconvenience is a small enough price to pay."

CCOM board member and attorney Hal Lary negotiated for Lindley to obtain occupancy of the house for a number of years. He started negotiations with a 99-year occupancy. That was the standard agreement when the federal government took control of the homes which would become a part of the Cape Cod National Seashore. The settlement worked out by Lary was for an occupancy of 35 years, according to Carol Morrison. (Morrison remarked on the irony that Hilda Lindley died of cancer a mere seven years after the settlement was worked out.)

"My mother gave up her house—her only asset and her favorite place on earth—to preserve this land," lamented John Lindley.

"Hilda had intelligence, energy and political savvy," recalls former CCOM President Richard Johnson. "She was often tearful when she went before the county in pleading to save both Indian Field and her home. At one point, she involved Charles Lindbergh, whose several books she had helped publish when she worked for Harcourt Brace. Not only did he address the County Legislators, but he put his arm around Hilda to comfort her when she was visibly upset."

As John Lindley recalls it:

> There were an incredible series of events. My mother had been working for the *New York Times Book Review*, and a friend suggested the eviction would make an important story. It landed on the front page of the Saturday *New York Times*. The condemnation of the house, presented as policy, was in reality a vindictive act. It caught the eye of Senator James Buckley, a conservative and a Libertarian. He was incensed, and called my mother to offer help. He hooked her up with Dan Mahoney, an attorney who then represented her. He knew "the Albany guys" in the game. He negotiated with the county for acceptable terms, and afterward refused to take her money.

A *New York Newsday* column in September of 1973 by William F. Buckley, Jr. (brother of Senator James Buckley) was headlined DEFENDING A BLOCKHOUSE IN EASTERN SUFFOLK. It fell perfectly in line with Buckley's libertarian political position. He described it as "a human story, the individual against the state." Buckley noted the blockhouse had been bought,

> ...for the peanuts it was worth by Mrs. Hilda Lindley, a young woman whose marriage broke up a few years later. There, without alimony or help of any kind from anyone, Mrs. Lindley spent every weekend with her three children, leaving to go to work in a publishing house in New York City on the 5:30 A.M. train on Mondays. She saved every penny she earned, sent her children to fine schools, and built up her beloved blockhouse and, in her spare time, importuned the elders of Suffolk County to take over the adjacent 800 acres as part of the land bank program.
>
> She must have argued the case very eloquently, because said elders suddenly felt the acquisitive imperative, and decided a year

A fresh water lake, Big Reed Pond (foreground), and a brackish lake, Oyster Pond (center) are home to huge populations of migrating waterfowl. Big Reed is in Theodore Roosevelt County Park, and Oyster Pond forms the western boundary of Montauk Point State Park.

or so ago to take over not only the 800 acres of wild land, but also the two acres that belonged to poor Mrs. Lindley.

Buckley concluded with this caveat to the county:

> If they say no [to Lindley's plea for reciprocal privilege], they had better watch out.... When the agents come to take it, they will perish under a rain of arrows shot through the machicolations of Mrs. Lindley's dream house by her friends, who will gather there to make the point that even as in the past the price of liberty was eternal vigilance against German submarines, now the price is vigilance against unfeeling gentlemen from the County Legislature.

The editor notes that this was sent by Buckley to Dan Mahoney, the lawyer John Lindley mentioned who was also chair of the New York State Conservative Party.

"People were saying terrible things about Hilda. That all she wanted was to live in her house surrounded by a park. They also didn't like the fact that she was a woman [initiating this]. One time she came back to Montauk and found some of her windows had bullet holes in them," Lillian Disken recalls.

The January 1973 CCOM newsletter included this commentary after Lindley's occupancy agreement had been finalized:

> Mrs. Lindley wishes to thank all CCOM members who helped her so generously in this six-week struggle, particularly the members of the executive board who gave so unstintingly of their time, money and presence. Her victory is a wonderful demonstration that people working together are stronger than any single individual, and in saving her home we see another example of the impossible being achieved—the same impossible that some skeptics predicted when we set out to save Indian Field from the rape of the bulldozers.

CCOM Incorporates

In July of 1971, with the help of attorney Joseph Duffy, the CCOM executive board met to approve recasting itself as a not-for-profit corporation. Such a designation meant being unable to take political stands. Duffy advised leaving that to individuals, and instead making statements based on "information and belief." CCOM has assiduously followed that advice to this day. As a result, when board members have run for political office or held politically appointed positions from either party—members such as Helen Sarvis, Richard Johnson, Russell Stein, and Lisa Grenci—they resigned their CCOM organizational offices.

"Our focus has always remained environmental and not political," states Richard Johnson. Citing the 6,000 votes the organization got out during the critical time with Indian Field, and the 15,000 letters that would be sent to Washington several years later protesting offshore oil drilling near Montauk, Johnson summarized the group's approach: "We were never a political party, but we knew how to use politics to get our end."

From the first, Hilda Lindley sought alignments with other organizations, including the East End Council of Organizations (EECO). That organization included The Baymen's Association, The Nature Conservancy (TNC), and the Ladies' Village Improvement Society (LVIS). Kay Dayton, who became CCOM representative to the EECO, observed that "Every little corner of the Hamptons seemed to erupt into a group like us." For instance, in 1970 a suit against the Town concerning Indian Field was joined with the Suffolk County Defenders of the Environment, the Preservation Society of the East End, and the Springs Civic Association. There would be more suits to come.

The mission statement at the time of incorporation as a not-for-profit organization read:

- To preserve the environment and ecology of Montauk.
- To support and aid projects which benefit and preserve the natural resources of Montauk.
- To apprise the citizens and governing bodies of the necessity and duty under the law to protect and preserve the water, land, air and wildlife of Montauk.
- To propose and support legislation which will enhance, promote, and foster the preservation of the environment and ecology of Montauk.
- To enlist the aid of the governing bodies and the courts to enforce those existing laws which pertain to the preservation of the environment and ecology of Montauk.

When the group incorporated in that important month of July, it also embarked upon a major membership drive. In the letter she included with a clip-out membership form, Hilda Lindley wrote:

In one short year we have already accomplished many things that most people said couldn't be done:
- Helped save Indian Field from developers' bulldozers for a county park.
- Persuaded the Town to take action in cleaning up Ditch Plains Trailer Park, long a community eyesore.
- Succeeded in stepping up the program of policing Town waters.

• Attended every East Hampton Town meeting to present our members' views on matters of concern to Montauk.

• Conducted monthly public meetings at which qualified speakers have informed the community on vital issues.

• Published a monthly newsletter alerting our members to matters of current concern.

• Provided an organization which can get action on matters that might often be difficult for one individual to achieve.

Therein reads a testament to the work achieved "in one short year" by this small, energetic group of Montauk environmentalists and their dynamic president, Hilda Lindley.

HILDA'S HAND-ME-DOWNS

Ever since its inception, CCOM has abided by the philosophy and principles of Hilda Lindley. In shorthand, they are *Hilda's Hand-Me-Downs*:

• Members are encouraged to attend all governmental town meetings—Town Board, Planning Board, Zoning Board.

• Members should read the local papers, especially the legal notices about development applications, official notifications of Town plans, etc.

• Members should be prepared to speak up and be active at Town meetings.

• CCOM will take legal action as necessary—lawsuits can be used as a final weapon in CCOM's fighting arsenal.

• Board members must be prepared to travel to Albany and/or Washington D.C. to lobby lawmakers about environmental concerns.

• Hold public forums on environmental topics to educate the public.

• Facilitate political discussion before each Election Day through an annual Meet the Candidates event.

• Do community outreach and participate in the community through public events like Earth Day, Field Day, and the local school's environmental programs, etc.

• Recruit environmentally responsible members of the community to CCOM's Board of Directors.

• Have parties!

DID SOMEBODY SAY PARTY?

20th ANNUAL SUMMER GALA. DINING, DANCING. MUSIC BY "THE HITMAN,"
PAUL NICHOLS, EAST HAMPTON'S MOST POPULAR DJ. JUNE 26, 5 TO 7:30PM.
THIRD HOUSE — MONTAUK COUNTY PARK. $25 TAX DEDUCTIBLE DONATION
BENEFITS THE MONTAUK ENVIRONMENT. TICKET INFORMATION 668-2282.

CONCERNED CITIZENS OF MONTAUK, INC.
PO BOX 915, MONTAUK

Chapter 2

Open Space: Major Battles to Save the Land

T HE BATTLE TO SAVE INDIAN FIELD was the impetus for the formation of CCOM, and once the organization was up and running, it became clear that a major focus of its activities would become the preservation of open space.

The building boom was beginning to transform Montauk, and as the 1970s drew to a close, development throughout the Eastern end of Long Island was launching into high gear. THE SOUTH FORK IN CRISIS, declared a headline in the November 21, 1982 issue of the *East Hampton Star*. "East Hampton is under the most intense development pressure in its almost 325-year history as a town. It is undergoing perhaps as all-encompassing a change as was the arrival in 1648 of the first white settlers."

The *Montauk Pioneer* went even further with this topic. "Driving down Emerson Street along the water in the center of town, a longtime resident of Montauk expressed total disorientation. Was he in Fort Lauderdale? The condominium section of a Hawaiian island? In just a year, this particular part of downtown Montauk was totally unrecognizable from the year before." The article was written by Dan Rattiner, who cited the two previous building booms: Carl Fisher's develop-

SIXTEEN

DISCOVER HOW
UNFRIENDLY
MONTAUK CAN BE.
BUY THIS LAND.

LAST WEEK'S AUCTION of the Montauk Air Force Station drew protests from East Hampton Town residents, who pick-   RAV FREIDEL, a Montauk resident,
eted in front of the Manhattan offices of the General Services Administration before the bidding. The 278-acre site went for   was among the picketers.
$1.9 million, but the fate of the property still hinges on the outcome of a court case brought by the Town and State seeking
to block any transfer into private hands.

CCOM pickets outside the GSA office in New York City in 1984...

ment of downtown Montauk in 1926–29, the rush of motel building in 1952–56, and now the boom of the early 1980s. "How long would it last, anyway?" he asked.

Even the *New York Times* picked up on the issue: ONCE-SLEEPY MONTAUK FIGHTS TO SLOW DOWN DEVELOPMENT, ran a lead story in its Metropolitan Report. It described the 30,000 plague-ridden soldiers returning from Teddy Roosevelt's 1898 Cuban invasion, arriving in Montauk in August of that year to find a desolate fishing village. "Eighty-six years later, this village is once again scrambling to survive an influx of newcomers. But the wave of new arrivals is armed with dollars instead of guns, and carries condominium conversion plans instead of infectious diseases."

The members of CCOM had already seen the warning signs. As the 1980s got underway, the group spearheaded some of the fiercest—and most important—battles to save open space in Montauk.

Camp Hero

Spread across the top of page 16 of the February 16, 1984 issue of the *East Hampton Star* are three photos that tell a dramatic story. The first

THE EAST HAMPTON STAR, EAST HAMPTON, N.Y., FEBRUARY 16, 1984

JACK WEPRIN, at left, a Manhattan lawyer representing Joshua Sundance Inc., was the high bidder for the property. His $1.9 million bid was considered by many observers to be far less than the GSA hoped to get for the land, which the agency had offered to the Town for $3.25 million.   Photos by Mike Becker/Alternatives Group

...the first step towards preserving what is now Camp Hero State Park.

(above left) shows a group of picketers bundled against the obvious cold in front of an urban setting. The caption reads:

> Last week's auction of the Montauk Air Force Station drew protests from East Hampton Town residents, who picketed in front of the Manhattan offices of the General Services Administration [GSA] before the bidding. The 278-acre site went for $1.9 million, but the fate of the property still hinges on the outcome of a court case brought by the town and state seeking to block transfer into private hands.

The photo on the right identifies Jack Weprin, a Manhattan lawyer representing Joshua Sundance, Inc. (an Alaskan company), the highest bidder for the property. Notes the caption, "His $1.9 million bid was considered by many observers to be far less than the GSA hoped to get for the land, which the agency had offered to the Town for $4.5 million."

Between the two photos is another with the caption "Rav Freidel, a Montauk resident, was among the picketers." The sign he holds says, "DISCOVER HOW UNFRIENDLY MONTAUK CAN BE. BUY THIS LAND."

Fronting on the Atlantic Ocean only a quarter-mile from the Montauk lighthouse, Camp Hero is truly one of the most unique pieces of

U.S. GOVERNMENT
AUCTION

- Auction date scheduled for February 8, 1984.
- The former Montauk Air Force Station (278 Acres/Land and Buildings)
- Located at tip of Long Island, surrounded three sides by water and the bone property.
- from New York City by car.
- Credit terms available.
- The site is equipped (in 'as is' conditions) with water supply and distribution system, sanitary sewer system, other utilities.

U.S. General Services Administration For information call (212) 264-2650 or (617) 223-2651

Wednesday, February 8, 1984 • 11:00 AM
Room 112, 26 Federal Plaza
New York, NY

Literature announcing the auction of Montauk Air Force Station in 1984.

property on the east coast. Two rocky points and coves are the location for some of the best striped bass fishing in the country and also, particularly in September and October, some of the best surfing waves north of Puerto Rico. Moving inland, towering hoodoo bluffs give way to a virgin holly and laurel forest segmented by streams and home to a thriving wildlife population. In spring and fall thousands of migrating land birds and waterfowl pass through the Camp Hero expanse. In a small area of the middle of the property is an old military radar station and gun emplacements. And one huge abandoned radar tower is visible from almost anywhere in Montauk, but it is so well-built that the cost to remove it is prohibitive.

Russell Stein, who at that time was working as Town Attorney, described some of the background on the complicated situation.

> For 50 years the federal government had a policy of giving away surplus land, to the locality in which it was situated, for a dollar! That's what they did until 1980 when Reagan came in and Stockman, the budget guy... changed the policy.... Everybody assumed that when the Army and the Air Force left, [Camp Hero] would go to the county, the state, or the town for a dollar.

The State and Town plans to acquire the land of government surplus, and offer some 27 units of affordable housing at the base to local families, was an on-and-off affair. The November 11, 1982 *Star* records this description of a planning meeting at Town Hall, which included representatives of Senator Alfonse D'Amato's office, the Long Island State Parks Commission, the Suffolk County Development Corporation, Federal Office of Housing and Urban Development (HUD), East Hampton Town Supervisor Mary Fallon, and John Sheridan, general manager of the Long Island State Parks Commission: "Speaking to the General Services Administration's offer to the State and Town to make the first bid on the land, John Sheridan said, 'You people are morally bankrupt. You are paying off your debts with your assets.' He then went on to announce the State's intention to sue. 'The attitude is the public be damned.... Where the hell do you think the State will come up with the money?'" The story goes on to describe Sheridan's warning that "the Senator [D'Amato] better get involved before some guy will be putting up 100 condominiums here." Senator Daniel Moynihan, following a conversation with Town Councilman Tony Bullock, had excoriated the GSA on the floor of the Senate for selling property for development next to a "national monument—the Montauk Lighthouse." So incensed was he that he interrupted a speech by Senator Strom Thurmond.

On February 11, 1983, Secretary of the Interior William P. Clark entered the fray, writing that he favored preservation of the acreage as a park. (Kay Dayton stated that she had access to a contact who got the attention of Clark.) The letter to the GSA was received a day before the auction, but the federal government still planned to "proceed down a path toward a sale of the property," according to Carroll Jones, head of the GSA's Federal Property Resource Service.

Russell Stein recalls that "All the lawyers researched it (me, Dudine and others), and what we found was that the Stockman policy was certainly illegal. The change [of status] hadn't gone through Congress." The lawyers claimed that the auction was in violation of the National Environmental Policy Act and the Federal Coastal Zone Management Act, as well as the guidelines of the Federal Property Review Board.

Stein explains that "We got a restraining order in front of Judge [Leonard] Wexler.... That was the greatest hearing when some lawyer from the Justice Department got up and said, 'My orders in this case come from the highest levels of government.' Judge Wexler said, 'I don't care if your orders come from Pluto, young lady, I will decide in this case!'"

Because the sale had been advertised and bidders were coming from everywhere, "Wexler crafted this Solomonic decision.... The judge said: 'I'll let you have your auction, but you can't convey title. Before you start your auction you have to say there's a major lawsuit underway with substantive claims.'... I don't think Wexler wrote a final decision. It never got to the next level. The GSA backed off.... The Suffolk County Legislature was in an uproar. They had a 70-year-old public park and they [the Federal government] were giving it away to a guy from Alaska to build condos! Eventually the pressure became so great that D'Amato called the White House and said, 'I'm getting killed here. Please, just sell it to the Town and sell another piece in Nevada, okay?' That's how these things get settled. So one day the Feds called us up and said, 'It's yours. You can have it for one dollar!' The lawsuit was crucial in pumping it up."

Acknowledging that the selling of Camp Hero was the issue that drew him to CCOM, Rav Freidel describes his participation at that auction. "It was a freezing cold day. I took it upon myself to show up to protest the selling of Camp Hero by the GSA... The government wanted $4.5 million for the property and the Town didn't want to buy it. I called the GSA and said, 'How can you sell it? This is where George Washington built the lighthouse. It's where all our ancestors passed on the way to Ellis Island and New York Harbor. This property, you can't sell it!'"

Upon discovering there would be an auction, Freidel had signs made up for himself and his wife, Sandy, and they went to Federal

Camp Hero, with abandoned radar tower (center), covers the south coast west of Montauk Point Lighthouse and Turtle Cove.

CAMP HERO

The area called Camp Hero borders the Sanctuary on its western boundary. A portion of the property was once used as a military base, however, the majority of the parcel is a natural wildlife habitat, with extensive beaches, woodlands, and wetlands. Many extraordinary species of flora and fauna, such as rare strands of Montauk moorlands, are sheltered here. It is also an extremely important part of the Great Eastern Flyway. On the tip of the island the park offers visitors a taste of near-wilderness by the sea. From the 80-foot coastal bluffs visitors can see Block Island 15 miles to the east, and below the rocky beach is an excellent surf casting location.

Plaza. "There was a whole bunch of people from CCOM. At that time I called them the 'Gray Panthers.' It was the Kay Carleys, the Carol Morrisons, the Diskens, the people we all know who have been doing this forever.... About 20 people [were] on the picket line. We got on the picket line. That was our introduction to CCOM. There was Dick Johnson, Bob Guarino, and Mike Albronda [the captain of a charter boat in Montauk] and [Broadway producer] Norman Kean. Here I was walking around in a suit chanting 'GSA go away' and 'Don't let the White House sell the Lighthouse.'"

Putting away their signs and leaving the 10-degree cold and wind to enter the auction room, Freidel tells this anecdote:

> We were raising our hands and asking questions trying to get in the way.... Richard Johnson had a Nehru jacket on and the head of the auction pointed to him and said, "The good father would like to say something." He thought he was a priest, so they even thought we brought priests out to save the property! The bids were so low they knew they were not going to get the $4.5 million.

In the end there was a land swap. The Federal government got property they wanted at Fire Island as part of the National Seashore Recovery Act while New York State got Camp Hero. For this success Freidel credits what the *East Hampton Star* called "the unusual coalition of environmental groups and hunting and sports fishing lobbies" that was formed to organize Island-wide opposition to the sale.

Gus and Doris Ruhle (parents of Tom Ruhle, who would become a Town Councilman) were part of the picket line. Commenting on the final disposition of the case, Ruhle said, "I think because the State thought it [the selling of the Air Force Base] was a stupid idea and CCOM made such an organized effort, they worked out a compromise where they had a face-saving deal [for the federal government]." The 278 acres became a part of Montauk State Park.

"That was the first big piece of open space gotten in a long time," recalls Larry Penny. "That was before [the struggle to preserve East Hampton's] Barcelona Neck, before Hither Woods. That really set the stage. All those pieces of open space we wanted to secure, that was the big one, the first since Theodore Roosevelt County Park." But though

The Old and New Rt. 27 split right in the center of Hither Hills State Park, established by Robert Moses in 1924.

this initial victory was important, securing open space is not necessarily the same as preserving it—as will be shown, this was only part one of the battle for Camp Hero.

Hither Woods

Prior to the formation of CCOM it seemed that no one, including the Town departments charged with oversight, was looking too hard at the consequences of the rush to subdivide and build motels. According to former Assistant Town Attorney Richard (Rick) Whalen, in 1968 the Curtiss–Wright Corporation proposed to develop 5,000 homes in Hither Woods, a parcel of more than 1,300 wooded areas just north of the Hither Hills State Park land preserved by Robert Moses. It borders Napeague Harbor and Gardiners Bay. "They didn't pursue it very hard, so it petered out," he said. There was a "Wild West" mentality toward Montauk at the time—an attitude of "anything goes" and "make your

With Goff Point and Napeague Harbor in the foreground, Hither Hills State Park includes the famous "Walking Dunes" where Rudolph Valentino's *Sheik of Arabia* was filmed.

own rules." That philosophy continues to a lesser degree even today. As current CCOM President Bill Akin says, "In Montauk there has always been a philosophy of: Do it! We'll worry about the consequences later. That has proven to be a very viable business strategy."

The need to preserve the Hither Woods parcel was brought to the attention of CCOM by John Gosman. Subsequently, Russell Stein, representing the Group for the South Fork, and Carol Morrison, representing CCOM, went to a meeting with the State Parks Commission to lobby for monies to purchase two separate parcels, one of which bordered Napeague Harbor. The other was Hither Woods. The Napeague parcel Stein argued for did receive funding, while the Hither Woods parcel CCOM argued for did not.

Whalen was another driving force behind the push to save Hither Woods. His interest was whetted in college, when he read Everett Rattray's book *The South Fork*. He was intrigued by the Montauk place names like Eli's Run, Split Rock, and the Devil's Cradle. Whalen found work in Montauk, and he also found pleasure in running on the beaches and walking in the wilderness areas. He says:

Including (clockwise from left) Hither Hills State Park (1924), Hither Woods Preserve (1986), and Suffolk County Preserve (1988), a huge portion of forest, lake, and dune area borders Block Island Sound just west of the Montauk hamlet.

I remember in August of '79 going for a walk in Hither Woods with my three brothers. We started on the railroad tracks near the end of Navy Road. We'd just walk the tracks, that's how we got in…. You had the woods roads, the powerlines, and the railroad tracks. I remember it was a rainy, drizzling day. We walked as far as Quincetree landing. I remember looking to the woods to the south from the railroad embankment and you could see some [great] distance. It made a big impression. It was like looking into a jungle—lush, green summertime. Once I learned where Hither Woods was I began to run back there, which led me to begin to map the trails, at least in a rough way. I began to love that area—how unique it was… It was my idea of Montauk's wilderness.

By 1980, Whalen had become environmentally interested and active. He spoke at Planning Board meetings, and was a supporter of what the Democratic majority on the Town Board was doing to advance East Hampton's environment, including the Farmland Preservation Law and "a lot of innovative things."

Fresh Pond, the Walking Dunes, and Napeague Harbor are ecological treasures preserved by Hither Hills State Park.

Whalen characterizes the Democratic losses of every vacant seat in the 1981 election as having been "a shock" to anyone involved in East Hampton environmental issues. Two weeks after the election, when visiting the Ruhle family (his college friend Tom Ruhle was a bayman and Montauk native), Tom's father Gus Ruhle told him there was a rumor that the Republicans were going to abolish the Town planning department. Recalls Whalen,

> I thought the town was going to be destroyed... There was a lot of vacant land in town, and subdivision activity was very heavy... What people didn't realize was that there were a lot of people under the skin of that government that wanted to make the maximum amount of money out of the town and then leave.... There were people who thought the best use of the town's shoreline... was a high density resort development, such as you might see further south or in Florida....
>
> I knew it [Hither Woods] was a very special place; it was the largest undeveloped land out here.

A few weeks after the 1981 election, Whalen was returning from the Ruhles' house.

> There was a full moon and I remember driving along the highway near Hither Woods and thinking, we've got to do something to preserve Hither Woods.... If we preserve that land, in conjunction with Hither Hills State Park, we'd know that whatever happens we'd at least have a gigantic preserve with a beautiful coastline that would remain forever pristine. Within a matter of weeks, Tom Ruhle and I decided we were going to try to initiate a way to get public money to buy and preserve that land.

"There were five of us," said Tom Ruhle. "Rick Whalen, CCOM President Dick Johnson, Russell Hoeflich [then Director of the Nature Conservancy], Russell Stein, and me. And we said: form a coalition for Hither Woods!" Their task was a huge one: many people in Montauk thought there were plenty of woods and didn't understand the intense need to save more of them.

Whalen recalls,

> It was going to be an assemblage of people and organizations. The basic organizations were CCOM and the Group for the South Fork.... Charlene Briand.... was tremendously energetic and I cannot overstate how important she was. Carol Morrison was very involved; Russell Stein was essentially the legal mind; Larry Penny was peripherally involved.... One of the first things we did was draft a letter with variations to the newspapers.... We went around even driving to the North Fork to drop off copies of the letter for publication, to Riverhead, Southold, we went to the whole East End, everywhere.

Ruhle recounted more of the early days of the Coalition's work:

> There was also the argument [we made] about the groundwater sitting under Hither Woods.... We... wrote letters and we got the Town to put up a bond referendum; [they were] hoping that if it lost, we'd go away. The voters didn't care; they wanted to buy this.[1]

The Coalition then went to other agencies and told them that East Hampton had committed money to the acquisition by referendum. Gregory Blass, Suffolk County Legislator, set up the Hither Woods Task Force, which included representatives of the Coalition for Hither Woods, CCOM, the Group for the South Fork, The Nature Conservancy, the Suffolk County Water Authority, County Legislator Patrick Heaney, Blass, and other state officials. "John Behan [State Assemblyman] kept saying: these people are dreaming," Ruhle said. "He said he was for it, but it wouldn't happen. Blass, a Republican, was great; he got others involved."

The history of preserving the Hither Woods parcel of 1,357 acres is complex. The property was initially owned by the Benson Estate, which sold it to several developers.[2]

In 1972 Curtiss–Wright split the property. The northern part of 580 acres was acquired by George Semerjian, president of Levon Properties Corporation, which had been a subsidiary of Curtiss–Wright in 1967, according to an article in the *East Hampton Star* of June 8, 1972. It was the site of a defunct sand mining operation by the former owners, Long Island Aggregate, from whom Curtiss–Wright had bought the property in 1966.

Semerjian was "a big player in East End development since at least the 60s. He was very active in Southampton Village," says Rick Whalen. An article in the *Star* dated March 3, 1973 noted that Semerjian was involved in "a highly controversial joint mining-development

---

1. In November 1982, East Hampton voters passed a $1.5 million bond issue for the preservation of Hither Woods by a 2-to-1 margin. Since then, Town officials have lobbied in Albany for State funding. (Source: *East Hampton Star*, December 2, 1982.)

2. Mary Benson and Thyrza Benson Fowler, the descendants of Arthur Benson, sold the property to Montauk Properties Investment Corporation on July 9, 1956. According to the deed dated July 1, 1963, the Hither Woods Property Investing Corp., Peninsula Property Investing Corp., and Fort Pond Property Investing Corp. (the party of the first part) sold it to the Long Island Aggregate Corporation. The property was deeded over to the Curtiss–Wright Corporation on August 18, 1966.

project he had undertaken with the Curtiss–Wright Corporation at Jamesport, and had later been forced by public and governmental pressure to abandon."[3]

The Jamesport controversy caused Curtiss–Wright to come under attack in Montauk after it proposed to develop a tract "with 4,000 housing units, some of which would have been built on bluffs in the CIH [Commercial Industrial Heavy] zone and MD [Multiple Dwelling] zones once they had been 'terraced' by sand and gravel," according to the *Star*. Opposition, primarily from a group called Citizens Concerned for East Hampton [sic], led to the tabling of the plan until the Town adopted a new zoning ordinance. When it did, in the mid-1970s, Curtiss–Wright sued the Town and lost.

Following the Jamesport episode and the division of the Curtiss–Wright property in Montauk into two separate parcels, a *Star* article quoted Semerjian as saying, "I won't have any partners this time." His company got all the waterfront along Block Island Sound, Curtiss–Wright all the interior of some 777 acres. That interior portion along the highway was eventually purchased for $4 million in 1982 by an "anonymous group" called Sun Beach Real Estate Development Corporation, who proposed to create 243 two-acre house lots, cluster 88 apartments in attached houses on the land, and put in a private golf course.

Semerjian's property, with Benson Point to the north and overlooking Block Island Sound, eventually devolved to the Toronto Dominion Bank of Canada and was then bought by the developers Dune Associates. It included all of the waterfront and the sand mining gravel pit. Forty acres of this land is now a Town Park. A proposal was made to put a 96-unit subdivision on 263 acres north of the Long Island Railroad (LIRR) tracks at Benson Point. This was the first subdivision in the Hither Woods area to come before the Planning Board.

"Unfortunately, we began our big push at the very end of 1981, the early part of winter, 1982," says Rick Whalen, commenting on the ironies of timing. "What we didn't know was that they [Curtiss–Wright]

---

3. The property was later sold to the Long Island Lighting Company (LILCO) in the mid-70s, which attempted to build a nuclear power plant successfully opposed by CCOM and other Long Island organizations.

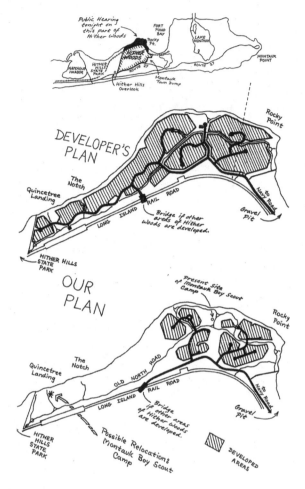

Developers' plans for Benson Point were well on their way to becoming a reality.

were looking to unload the property and had already found a buyer....
Apparently they had overseas investors, especially from Italy. It was a
corporation named Sun Beach Real Estate; its spokesman was a finan-
cier named Nicola Biase.... So, they bought the land." With some regret,
Whalen recalled learning after the fact that the president of Curtiss–
Wright had been active with The Nature Conservancy. "If there had been
a chance of getting some public money, they might have been a willing
seller. By the time we were ready to go, they were already in contract."

"The Economic, Political and Civic Aspects of Saving Hither Woods," was the topic addressed by Nancy Nagle Kelly of the Group for the South Fork, at CCOM's annual membership meeting in July, 1982. She urged a multi-pronged acquisition approach for preservation. The developers hired the consultant firm of Holzmacher, McLendon and Murrell to do the required groundwater survey. Their results stated that development would not compromise Montauk's water supply. This was challenged as being "premature" by environmentalist Larry Penny and others.

Also at the CCOM meeting, County Legislator Gregory Blass pointed out the dangers to the underground water supply and stressed both the need to preserve the acreage as a water-recharge area and for recreation, and the urgent need for action. The program included Rick Whalen's slide show of Hither Woods. "The financial situation of the Coalition is critical," stated CCOM President Richard Johnson, sounding the alarm.

Tom Ruhle, who was Chairman of the Coalition for Hither Woods, presented an update on the Coalition's progress at a CCOM board meeting on October 16, 1982. He explained that Dune Associates and Sun Beach Realty were suing the Town Board on the constitutionality of a Town moratorium on development of Hither Woods, based on the ruling against it by Judge George McInerney. As a result, Dune Associates was currently seeking automatic approval of their plans to build their subdivision. The Coalition was therefore joining the Town as intervenors. They hired David Neufeld as their lawyer and hoped to receive standing in the case. Rick Whalen remembered that Mildred Davis, CCOM's recording secretary who lived close to Hither Woods, became a plaintiff in the litigation.

Two scenarios were possible in trying to save Hither Woods. The best solution was that the Town, county, and state purchase the acreage. Short of that, clustered housing and an open space set-aside provision would be the lesser evil.

The hearing on the proposed development was held on October 28, 1982. IT'S JUST NOT FAIR FOR THE WOODS TO GO AWAY was the *East Hampton Star* caption under a photo of seventh-grader Louann Sylvia, who attended with 14 other Montauk school students. Larry Penny catalogued the environmental impacts to the crowd filling Town Hall. "The developers were mostly quiet, however," records the newspaper. When Dune Associates attorney and partner John McGowan rose to rebut, "groans greeted his summary of water studies when he stated: 'There's plenty of water in Montauk.'"

CCOM sponsored a money-raising series of nature walks during the Montauk Fall Festival that October. They were led by Larry Penny and Rick Whalen, and covered four locations: Montauk Point, the Montauk Moorlands, north of the Point at Oyster Pond, and Shadmoor. That same Fall Festival featured a tour of eight of Montauk's "exceptional" homes. They included the houses on Old Montauk Highway of Dr. William L. Curry, E. B. White, Maria Lubinska, Richard Johnson, and Dr. Howard Krieger, as well as one or two of the "Association" houses (houses built by Carl Fisher and designed by Stanford White).

Richard Johnson held a fund-raiser cocktail party at his home to raise the $10,000 needed to pay lawyers' fees and for an environmental consultant, while Kay Dayton contacted some foundations for financial support. CCOM members hand-addressed letters requesting contributions of $100 ($1,000 for those who could afford it), for the work. By July of 1983, $25,000 was raised toward litigation costs.

Richard Johnson (who became CCOM president in 1982) was forthright in his appeals, as evidenced by this letter to a foundation trustee:

Dear Mr. Ames:

The residents of the hamlet of Montauk... are making an enormous effort to save from development their last fresh water reservoir which underlies 1,350 acres of forested land called Hither Woods, adjacent to Hither Hills State Park. Today, we have a fleeting opportunity to be a community with an adequate, clean, water supply—permanently secured.

Concerned Citizens of Montauk, a non-profit organization of 600 members... is backing the efforts of ad hoc citizen groups which have formed to argue and negotiate for the property to be placed in public ownership.

We submit for your consideration a request for funds to help us attain a goal of $45,000 to defray the costs of litigation in this

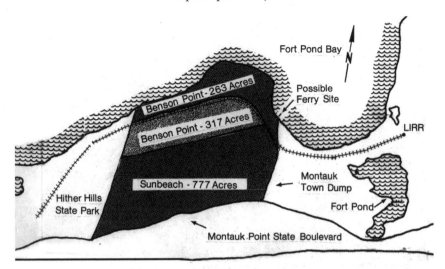

THE NORTHERN PART of Hither Woods, called Benson Point, will be the subject of Wednesday's East Hampton Town Planning Board hearing. One hundred units are proposed on the waterfront acreage. while the 317-acre interior portion would be put in a reserved area.

This is the best map showing the parcels of land that are discussed in this chapter. There were really two separate projects: Benson Point (a.k.a. Rocky Point) and Hither Hills (a.k.a. Sunbeach properties, Lee Koppelman Preserve).

effort.... The reason for the urgency we hope to convey with this letter is the recent action of our Town Planning Board. Despite the fact that a Town referendum last November received approval by the voters of East Hampton by two-to-one to make $1.5 million available by the Town towards the purchase... the Planning Board has now granted preliminary approval to the contract purchasers for subdivision of approximately 560 acres of the parcel....

CCOM urged its members to act by attending the Town Planning Board meeting on Hither Woods, by writing the appropriate authorities, and by contributing funding to the legal struggle. Because of its tax-exempt status, CCOM was able to collect money for the Coalition. The September 1982 newsletter reported that "Money will be needed to compensate expert witnesses for hours of work and testimony before the Planning Board and to pay for legal actions to protect the public interest in the Hither Woods reservoir."

Just before the November 2, 1982 vote on Proposition II, Larry Penny devoted a comprehensive, educational full page in the *East Hampton Star* to Hither Woods. He described its history, starting with the Montaukett Indians who viewed it as hallowed ground; he also included descriptions of its geology, its aquifer, its flora and fauna, and its endangered species.

The urgent tone of the fundraising appeal to CCOM's membership is apparent. Matters became even more crucial when a lower court declared that East Hampton's 90-day moratorium on development in Hither Woods was illegal, and that the East Hampton Town Board ignored overwhelming public pressure to appeal the decision and discouraged efforts to put together a coalition of Town, county, state, and the SCWA to fund the purchase of the development called Benson Point. By November 1983 the CCOM newsletter reported that all three sections of Hither Woods were tied up in the courts:

Benson Point—Section I. Hither Woods Coalition of which CCOM is a member has sued the Town Planning Board for its approval of the proposed preliminary map.... The Planning Board can take no further action while this development is in litigation.

Benson Point—Section II. The developers have sued the Planning Board for default of action and thereby claim automatic approval of the preliminary map.... At the request of the Planning Board, the developer submitted a Draft Environmental Planning Statement. Again the Planning Board cannot act because of litigation.

Sun Beach Hills. Both the Town Planning Board and the County Planning Commission have denied approval of the preliminary map for this development. Justice George McInerney gave a favorable decision to the developers when they sued the Planning Board for defaulting on taking action on the preliminary map. This gave the developers automatic approval for their map.... This time the Town has appealed the decision before the Appellate Division of the New York State Supreme Court.

Commenting on the Hither Woods situation, Russell Stein reported that Hither Woods "became the lightning rod. That's where the lawsuit gets

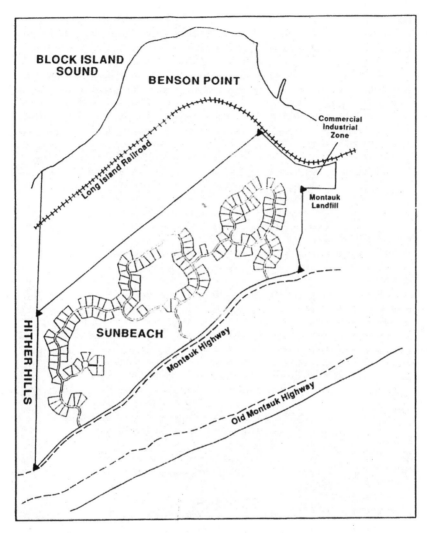

The Sunbeach plans for Hither Hills would have seen almost 400 houses on what is now known as the Koppelman Preserve.

written, all the guerilla warfare gets waged. It went on for five years." He recalled being asked during the course of a three-hour deposition whether he was a member of CCOM. "I am," he replied. "And not only that, I am a card-carrying member of CCOM." He got out his wallet and showed it to them. He viewed the line of questioning as implying that CCOM was running the town. "I remember I kept thinking, I wish CCOM *were* running the town, and it's not even close." (The previous administration had fired Planning Department head Tom Thorsen and abolished the Planning Department. They then hired development-oriented consultants Rochis Associates to oversee all planning in the Town.)

By 1984, with the Democrats regaining control of the Town Board, the political situation improved. Rick Whalen credits the Democratic win for saving Hither Woods. Included on the new Planning Board was former CCOM President Helen Sarvis; Russell Stein became the newly appointed Town Attorney. With the shift in power these and many other players created the 1984 Comprehensive Plan, which instituted major changes in Montauk's zoning requirements. A moratorium on development was declared, and Stein drafted an entirely new Town zoning code with much tougher requirements for open space. Wetlands were given special attention, with new laws requiring most development to obtain new environmental "special permits."

"It was a pretty wild year," Whalen says. "Some big, powerful developers opposed them every step of the way." When queried as to their identity, Whalen named Ben Heller, Frank Dragotta, and Nicola Biase, all developers. "There were attorneys litigating almost everything the new Town Board did."

Following a public hearing on December 18, 1984, the Town adopted the new zoning code. Because the new code had to be filed with the Secretary of State, "they adopted it that morning at a Town Board meeting, and flew it to Albany to be filed that day," Whalen recalls, adding to the drama that accompanied the political shifts that year. "They were taking no chances." The new zoning code disrupted the development plans for Hither Woods, which were still up in the air.

Despite the new Democratic Town Board and the sweeping new changes, the legal battles over Montauk's open space continued. CCOM and the Coalition hired David Neufeld to challenge Planning Board development approvals on State Environmental Quality Review Act (SEQRA) grounds.[4] With two major subdivision applications adjoining one another on such a large part of Montauk, Neufeld argued, protecting the water supply and the ecology necessitated a DEIS (Draft Environmental Impact Statement), which the pre-1984 Planning Board had not required. "That lawsuit was successful," said Rick Whalen. "It's very hard for a citizen's group to beat a municipal agency in court, but

KEEP THE WOODS IN HITHER WOODS.

CCOM's "Keep the Woods in Hither Woods" bumper sticker.

Neufeld went before Supreme Court Judge Daniel Luciano. He found in favor of the Coalition and the other plaintiffs and threw out the Planning Board's preliminary approval, which... is the most important stage in the subdivision of a piece of property. It increases its value."

Like Russell Stein, Tom Ruhle was also sued in many legal battles. "I got sued seven times in my various official capacities, for various things that had to do with Mr. Biase's feeling of being mistreated by the Town." He was also sued by the Beachcomber motel developer for $62 million, "claiming that's what I cost him. [Ruhle was then a Town councilman]. The idea was to deplete the Town."

The strategy of depleting the Town's coffers with lawsuits was one that could have been disastrous for the future of Hither Woods—not to mention the rest of the important preservation issues facing Montauk. CCOM urged its members to attend public hearings and make the Planning Board aware of their concerns. Publicizing the struggle and alerting its membership, a flyer insert was placed in CCOM's newsletter in the winter of 1986:

KEEP THE WOODS IN HITHER WOODS!

Do you want public trails lost?

Do you want Navy Road to become a main traffic artery?

---

4. In adopting the State Environmental Quality Review Act (SEQRA) in 1978, it was the legislature's intention that all agencies conduct their affairs with an awareness that they are stewards of the air, water, land, and living resources, and that they have an obligation to protect the environment for the use and enjoyment of this and all future generations. Our greatest tool for preserving the quality of life in Montauk has been the SEQRA laws.

APPLAUSE for a long-fought battle to preserve Montauk's Hither Woods came after East Hampton Town Supervisor Judith Hope, left, signed a contract Monday for the Town to purchase 557 of its northern acres. Ms. Hope is flanked by Carol Morrison, president of the Concerned Citizens of Montauk, and Nancy Nagle Kelley, president of the Group for the South Fork.   *Joanne Furio*

Woods Contract Is Signed

East Hampton Town Supervisor Judith Hope (left), CCOM President Carol Morrison, and GSF President Nancy Nagle Kelley celebrate the purchase of 557 acres of Hither Woods in December 1986.

Do you want encroachment on a favorite beach?

Do you want pollution of our future water supply?

It was Russell Stein, Town Attorney under Supervisor Judith Hope, who was the "visionary thinker" (according to Larry Penny). His idea for saving the Hither Woods was revolutionary: rather than succumb to the developers, three government agencies—the Town, the county, and the state—could share in the purchase. That new paradigm was cited in *Newsday* article as "the nation's first joint open space acquisition by three levels of government." The *East Hampton Star* quoted CCOM President Carol Morrison as saying, "You can imagine my happiness and the happiness of all Concerned Citizens of Montauk members."

It took a good deal of involvement to make this three-pronged ownership plan work. Rick Whalen recalls that Maurice Hinchey was then a New York State Assemblyman in charge of the Committee on Environmental Conservation. "He became crucial in getting the state involved," Whalen says. "He came down and took a helicopter ride to look at the property. Without him, I don't believe Hither Woods state money could have been obtained." CCOM also made "Keep the Woods in Hither Woods" bumper stickers, ran ads in the local newspaper asking "Do you want your drinking water rain-fed or cesspool-fed?," and collected hundreds of petition signatures to present to the Town Board.

Tom Ruhle further describes the mechanics of the three-agency deal:

> The theory was that if you get two pieces of the puzzle, you could say to the third party: come on, you've got the county, you've got the Town, you'll get this property for half price. Russell's major contribution was the sharing, a new paradigm.[5]
>
> We simply put everything together. In fact the Sun Beach piece, there's actually Water Authority money in there. We said to them: you're the ones to pump water out of the ground so you have some interest in having something other than a two-acre well with a fence around it with a fertilized lawn on top…. They finally agreed to buy the northern piece from Dune Associates and the state was particularly interested in it because of the water. It was next to Hither Hills State Park, so it was a logical extension. They got it for half price…. It was a win–win situation. That was the first time for [a] purchase by multiple agencies."

The Water Authority eventually contributed $1 million to the acquisition of Hither Woods. The agency's plan for the area was to drill six new wells, three wells on the east side of the property and three on the western side, tapping into the aquifer. "Their wells usually are 250–300 feet [deep]. Hither Woods was identified as a watershed area and its potential for water was extremely high," says Carol Morrison. She reveals that the SCWA never proceeded, having done some testing and finding there was too much iron in the water. Apparently a decision was made that "it was cheaper to bring in that pipeline than to put in the filters…. One of the conditions of bringing in the pipeline was that

---

5. This paradigm was to govern the approach to preserving land in East Hampton in the following decades.

they develop those wells. But [as of 2005] they still haven't." (See Chapter 4 for more on the SCWA and the pipeline.)

When the zoning was changed and there were mandatory requirements for 50% open space in a development, it induced Dune Associates to negotiate. The purchase by the Town, county, and state of the 557 acres known as Benson Point I and II was made in 1986 for $4.5 million. The property "included almost two miles of waterfront," says Rick Whalen. "It didn't include the gravel pit piece... which was considered damaged land."

As Tom Ruhle tells it, John McGowan was the Dune Associates attorney and complained that his life had been made miserable. "He made a large profit from it and then he said, 'It was a very good Christmas that year,' and smiled," Ruhle said.

"It wasn't for another two years that the interior property was purchased," Whalen says. "Biase ultimately sold to the county in 1988." ("We were in court so often with Biase, he wouldn't sell it to the Town," Carol Morrison commented.) Whalen continued, "He got $17 million for it [777 acres]. We were overjoyed, anyway.... The Town now manages that property."

CCOM, and later even Nicola Biase, credit Dr. Lee Koppelman, the former director of the department and later executive director of the Long Island Regional Planning Board, as "instrumental in accomplishing the acquisition." And, according to a story run in the *East Hampton Star* regarding a transfer and dedication ceremony, Biase "lopped $1 million off the asking price when the county agreed to name the land after its former Planning Department director... whom Mr. Biase several times referred to as his 'idol.'... The property, which was sold without the Benson Reservations tied to it by deed, henceforth will be known as the Lee E. Koppelman Nature Preserve." The story mentions that the two men embraced before Mr. Koppelman took the dais to speak.

Says Rick Whalen, with evident pride and amazement,

> It [CCOM and the Coalition for Hither Woods] was the most successful ad hoc environmental group in the history of Long Island.... If we had known how hard the road would be, we'd have been seriously dissuaded from even trying. We were up against

It took two decades of persistent pressure from CCOM and finally cooperation by state, county, and Town governments, along with a big push from
The Nature Conservancy, to finally save Shadmoor's 99 acres between the
hamlet of Montauk and Ditch Plains.

very, very well-financed and well-connected developers on the
northern property; an extremely tough developer [Biase] on the
southern part.

Today, when one walks through the area known as Hither Woods, it's
hard to believe that just 20 years ago, this beautiful woodland was
zoned for heavy commercial and industrial use. "Can you imagine
that?" Whalen asks. "When you factor in the purchase of the last piece,
the gravel pit property... now a very popular Town park... 1,357 acres
have been preserved. The county has bought the 511 [Equities Corpo-
ration] property that lies east of the landfill... Today you have more
than 3,000 acres of contiguous land at Hither Woods, from the State
Park and some land the Town and state has purchased at Napeague
Harbor Road, added to all the properties. It's just incredible!"

Shadmoor

> Shadmoor has always been a kind of spiritual place for a lot of
> people who live out here, particularly those who live near it. You
> can walk through Shadmoor from Ditch Plains to the hamlet's cen-
> ter. You get this wonderful feeling up there on that property of the
> ocean and ragged coastline.

So says current CCOM President Bill Akin. He had helped to further the
acquisition of this unique parkland by inspiring the community to a dramatic moment of advocacy that culminated over 20 years of diligent
work by CCOM to have it purchased by the Town, county, and state.

Like the story of many large acquisitions, the one about Shadmoor
has a long, circuitous history. Commented former CCOM President
Dorothy Disken,

> I thought in 1980 I'd focus on pure environmental issues. I
> remember taking a walk [in Shadmoor] with Larry Penny. I'd
> always been afraid of heights. Larry discovered a plant there, say-
> ing, "You'll never see this again." To see the cliffs all undercut
> and have all the water coming through underneath—it was a
> learning situation for me.

The almost 99 acres of Shadmoor, which boasts a coastline frequently
described as one of the most dramatic in the state, is just east of the
center of Montauk. As Dorothy Disken implied, the area didn't appear
to be in danger in the early 1980s—at the time of the booming development craze, the fight to preserve Hither Woods was front and center in
the news. Yet in 1982, CCOM sponsored a group of educational fall
hikes to raise funds for Hither Woods preservation, and a hike to Shadmoor was included. The intent was to raise public awareness of Shadmoor's special properties, particularly the dramatic bluffs, which were
eaten away by erosion into fantastic forms called "hoodoos."

CCOM learned that the Town planning department had received an
application for Shadmoor for a subdivision of 66 units. Immediately
upon hearing of the threat of development, CCOM went into high gear,
notifying members of the Seaside Avenue Association and Surfside
Estates Association, groups that had been quite vocal on preserving

Shadmoor. Gwyda and Norman Kean of Surfside Estates personally hired William Jaeger, their own hydrologist, to map the wetlands, and John Klein became their lawyer of record. The groups pressed the Planning Board to mandate a Draft Environmental Impact Statement (DEIS) for the property. The area was a watershed area, considered part of the overburdened Oceanside/Ditch Plains drainage system, and there was concern about waste disposal, as drainage fed directly into Lake Montauk.

SHADMOOR

In 1982, one of the rarest plants in the world, sandplain gerardia (*Agalinis acuta)*, was discovered growing on a neglected grassy knoll in Shadmoor, the 100 acres of tableland along the cliffs just east of downtown Montauk. The more than 150 plants turned out to be the largest population in America in existence of this almost extinct plant. Along with a few other populations, this is the only remnant of a massive coastal *gerardia* population that once covered Montauk, producing a "sea of pink as far as the eye could see," as an early 20th century botanist put it.

Also flowering here are *arethusa*, a diminutive pink orchid, two rare ladies-tresses orchids, and seorse sedge. They are tucked in among a dwarf forest of shad, black cherry, winterberry holly and wind-clipped shrubs interlaced with small islands of maritime prairie. Part of what is called the Montauk Moorlands, it is a landscape characterized by a mosaic of miniature yet tough vegetation amid ponds and streamlets. The land falls abruptly to the sea on one side, and the face of this fall is precipitous, tortuously carved. Years of weathering have fluted the surface, leaving furrows flanked by sharp spines, so-called hoodoos. There are no other similar geological features along the entire Atlantic Coast of North America.

Shadmoor's heathland is also unlike any other on the Atlantic coast. When rain falls on Shadmoor, very little penetrates its clayey soil. So over the centuries the runoff has created a series of narrow sinuous channels, or ditches, that continue easterly to the aptly named Ditch Plain, after which it empties into Lake Montauk.

When the Town accepted the DEIS, CCOM engaged the services of InterScience Research to review it, and encouraged members to turn out for the public hearing. At the hearing, in January of 1983, CCOM recommended that the wetlands be mapped by the Department of Environmental Conservation (DEC) before a final "yield" of usable acreage was accepted. CCOM also proposed that a bluff line be established at the point of deepest erosion, along with a scenic easement setback, and that further study be done on drainage. The group also hired Larry Penny as a consultant for the mapping.

Meantime, the developers were digging wells for their development, which had to be approved by the health department. But Shadmoor's clay soils were not proving acceptable for septic systems. The Keans, actress Uta Hagen, and other neighbors noticed that the developers were trying to fudge the results of the well tests, and they reported this to the Town. At the hearing it was revealed that the developers were salting the wells. They were putting sand in them to show the county inspectors when they came that it was clean sand.

The developers withdrew their application when it was revealed that they had hit clay but tried to hide the fact by salting the wells. The DEC findings also indicated that "the [Shadmoor] wetlands are more extensive then previously depicted on the developer's maps," according to Larry Penny's report to CCOM. Penny said,

> They [the Planning Board] hadn't even mapped the wetlands yet for the [preliminary approval]. I came in with a wetland map... that blew the owners out of the water, because on their subdivision map they only had little teeny bits of wetlands and the one I brought to the hearing [showed that] the place was made up of a third covered with wetlands!

But the game was hardly over.

Activity by the owners of Shadmoor was dormant until the beginning of the 1990s, when a head of steam was building to preserve Shadmoor by CCOM, The Nature Conservancy, and a group called the Montauk Moorlands Association.[6] The owners came back before the Planning Board with an application to build 14 houses. An Action Alert went out in 1991 with a request that CCOM members write to

Two Town Supervisors: Jay Schneiderman and his predecessor, Cathy Lester, were both instrumental in the effort to save Shadmoor and several other parcels in Montauk.

Congressman George Hochbrueckner for federal money to help purchase the site. Though the acreage was targeted for acquisition by The Nature Conservancy and the U.S. Fish and Wildlife Service that year, the federal funding had not been forthcoming.

In 1993, the Planning Board deemed a DEIS prepared by the owners as "incomplete." William Esseks, their attorney, declared he would advise his clients to litigate. CCOM, along with The Nature Conservancy, were still pushing for the parcel to be preserved in its entirety. An endangered species called *sandplain gerardia*, one of the rarest

---

6. The Montauk Moorlands Association had been formed in 1982 by local residents and property owners in the Ditch Plains/Surfside area to protect the moorlands, starting with the Sanctuary.

plants in the world, was discovered growing in Shadmoor by Larry Penny. The extensive wetlands, possible archaeological significance, and visually stunning scenic vistas made a strong argument for acquisition. But the estimated asking price of $10 million for the undeveloped land was deemed "prohibitive" by the Town.

CCOM's newsletter of March 1994 was devoted to Montauk's open acres in need of preservation, including an eloquent description of Shadmoor by Larry Penny:

> What is to become of this extraordinary piece of geology with its bizarre forest composed of trees shorter than we are and its pockets of bluestem grassland fostering herbs that are rarer than rare? What of the hoodoos? The historic ditches? The receding bluffs and path? Surely Montauk, the Town of East Hampton, and, yes, even the world, stand much to gain from the [Shadmoor] of today, and much to lose should it become the Shad*less* of tomorrow.

Along with East Hampton Town Supervisor Cathy Lester and The Nature Conservancy's Stuart Lowrie, CCOM took this newsletter to Washington to lobby the Fish and Wildlife Congressional Committee for money to purchase the land. At a CCOM board meeting in April of 1995, President Rav Freidel reported that he had sent a letter to the U.S. Fish and Wildlife Department urging acquisition of Shadmoor. At a later meeting, Carol Morrison reported that the Town Board had also approved putting pressure on that federal department to commit funds for its purchase.

The pressure for acquisition was growing in intensity by 1996, as the Planning Board had approved the revised development plan by the owners. It further reduced the number of houses to four on approximately 12 acres each and a preserve area of 50 acres. Two potentially devastating conditions of the plan were that public access to trails would be denied and that the World War II bunkers on the property would be removed. The loss of public access in particular aroused public indignation, as the trails for hiking and biking were enjoyed by so many.

The bunkers were also prized as an historic part of Montauk. They had played an important role during the Second World War as observa-

WORLD WAR II bunkers are likely to be torn down as part of the development of Shadmoor. Tom Ruhle told the East Hampton Zoning Board of Appeals last week it would be a loss to history.   *Morgan McGivern*

A photo of the historic World War II bunkers from the *East Hampton Star*.

tion posts, and it was believed that they would be eligible to qualify for the National and State Registers of Historic Places. The *East Hampton Star* ran a story with a photo of CCOM board member and Open Space Committee chair Conrad Costanzo and former councilman Tom Ruhle standing in front of a bunker, expressing their consternation that the Planning Board had agreed to their removal.

Meanwhile, CCOM's board had debated a compromise proposal. It was put forth by the Group for the South Fork and advocated retaining public access and putting nine lots further back from the cliffs and clustering them together, instead of the developers' proposal to place four

SAVE SHADMOOR, SAVE THE TRAILS, SAVE THE BUNKERS

Residents and visitors:
Please help save Shadmoor by adding your name to those who would like to see the 99-acre Montauk moorland preserved for public use.

To the United States Fish and Wildlife Service; Bruce Babbitt, U.S. Sec. of the Interior; Gov. George E. Pataki:
Now is the time to re-appraise the 99-acre oceanfront parcel in Montauk, New York, known as Shadmoor for possible public purchase. The land is among the last large, unspoiled oceanfront natural habitats on Long Island. Its loss to private development would immeasurably diminish the quality of life for the thousands of residents and vacationers who visit the property every year. In addition, the two World War II-era observation bunkers on the property should be preserved as monuments to the region's involvement in that conflict.

The following businesses and organizations have joined in support of this petition: Concerned Citizens of Montauk, The East Hampton Star, East Hampton Trails Preservation Society, Group for the South Fork, Montauk Artists Association, Montauk Citizens Advisory Committee, Montauk Harbor Association, Montauk Lighthouse Museum, Montauk Youth, The Nature Conservancy, Surfside Estates.

CCOM supported this petition to federal and state authorities to save Shadmoor.

lots close to the cliff edge. CCOM's board took no action, as the organization's position continued to be for full acquisition of the acreage.

CCOM's Carol Morrison joined Town Supervisor Cathy Lester and Stuart Lowrie of The Nature Conservancy on a trip to Washington, D.C. in December of 1995. There they made a presentation to the U.S. House of Representatives Subcommittee on Fisheries, Wildlife, and Oceans in support of Congressman Michael Forbes' bill authorizing the U.S. Fish and Wildlife Service to acquire Shadmoor. The delegation then visited the offices of Senators Daniel Moynihan and Alfonse D'Amato, whose bill supporting federal funding for Shadmoor was awaiting a Senate floor vote. The group returned with some sense of optimism.

That summer CCOM's newsletter featured the headline SHADMOOR FUNDING EDGES CLOSER. Members read the good news that the Senate Appropriations Committee had approved an Interior Appropriations bill earmarking two million dollars toward purchase of the property. Congressman Forbes had worked hard on behalf of the acquisition, and was able to get the House of Representatives to pass his bill. It authorized the U.S. Fish and Wildlife Service to acquire Shadmoor. But, in a news article entitled "Sad Day For Shadmoor," the *East Hampton Star* reported that the monies that had been earmarked for the property, and "despite more than a year of lobbying, was usurped by Sterling Forest, a 20,000-acre watershed area on the New York–New Jersey border."

Senator Moynihan then wrote to Secretary of the Interior Bruce Babbitt to ask for funding. He noted that New York had received almost no federal funds to acquire land to protect endangered species: His letter continued,

> Last May 28th, the President signed P. L. 104-48, which authorizes the purchase of Shadmoor. Senator D'Amato and I introduced that legislation in the Senate and were pleased to see it become law. We were also informed that New York received $9 million in Land and Water Conservation Fund money for Sterling Forest. Shadmoor, however, was not funded.
>
> Both The Nature Conservancy and the Town of East Hampton are on record as willing financial partners. We need $2 million in federal funds to make this purchase. I ask that you provide whatever resources you have available to help with the addition of the Shadmoor property to the Amagansett National Wildlife Refuge.

Moynihan and the East End's federal representatives were unsuccessful in their efforts. However, there were other forces at work locally. The clock was ticking for Shadmoor, and the owners were becoming impatient after 15 years of ownership without developing their land. They had already begun constructing an access road on the property.

Town Supervisor Cathy Lester, conceding that the asking price of $17.3 million was "staggering," nevertheless pledged the Town's help to finish the purchase. The Town Board approved a $5 million bond issue toward the asking price. The Nature Conservancy also joined the effort with a $1 million contribution.

The *East Hampton Star* reported that the Town was working with County Legislator George Guldi and Assemblyman Fred Thiele on the state and county funding. Thiele had been pushing for preservation of the acreage for some time. "The state has shown a willingness in the past to add to its holdings in the Montauk area," he said. He was referring to monies spent toward the purchases of Hither Woods and Culloden (see the next section). He had been encouraged by his meetings with the governor's office and legislative leaders. Contributing funds toward the purchase would not require additional state legislation, as Shadmoor was listed as one of five or six priority pieces in the State Open Space Plan, and had already been approved for purchase. The state had set aside $500,000 for Shadmoor's purchase in 1998.

Meanwhile, Guldi had filed a bill in the County Legislature seeking two-thirds of the body's approval for authorization of a bond. He declared that "the upside is that we [the county] get the land preserved for one-third of the money; the downside is it's a lot of dollars." CCOM actively supported these efforts with meetings, attendance at hearings, and letters to all levels of government.

The singular event mentioned earlier, which rallied the Montauk community, took place on the imposing Shadmoor bluffs on an exquisite day early in October, 1999. This is the way Bill Akin describes what he calls "the single, most rewarding day" of his presidency:

> It all [the planning] took place in a week... at an annual [CCOM] meeting at Montauk. We always have an annual meeting with a subject which is interesting to people. That year the subject was Open Space. People from The Nature Conservancy came to speak and some from the Town. It was more or less a given that Shadmoor was going to be subdivided into four large lots. Access across that property that people had been hiking on for years, was going to be denied....
>
> Somebody [at the meeting] said, "Maybe we can save it. Why don't we do something?" I remember saying, "Well, if you're willing to support it, we'll do a rally next week!" I remember thinking,

THIS AERIAL PHOTO of the Shadmoor bluffs shows their unique erosion pattern. The group of people on the bluffs were part of a Save Shadmoor rally on Oct. 3.   *Doug Kuntz*

People arrived from all directions to protest the private development of "Shadmoor." One year later, it became a state park.

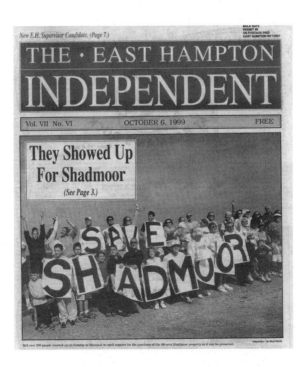

THE SECOND OF TWO formal events to commemorate the creation of Shadmoor State Park took place on its bluffs on Friday afternoon. With East Hampton Town Supervisor Jay Schneiderman at the podium, those taking part included Perry B. Duryea Jr., State Assemblyman Fred W. Thiele Jr., County Executive Robert J. Gaffney, County Legislator George O. Guldi, Town Councilmen Pete Hammerle and Job Potter, State Senator Kenneth P. LaValle, and Councilwoman Pat Mansir.   *Janis Hewitt*

The formal dedication ceremony of Shadmoor included a host of politicians who contributed to the preservation effort.

we will? Fortunately, the people got behind it. Someone I'd never met before—Debby Dolan, who is related to the Dolan family of cable television, who owned Channel 12 and all the cable system out here—came up and said, "I can give you media support." And I remember going downtown and Jimmy Hewett [a restaurant owner] said, "I'll get behind this 100%." We printed up posters that we're going to do a rally the next Sunday at 12 noon. We were going to have News 12 fly over. Just show up and show your support. The night before the rally, Lori Hensen, an artist visiting from Minnesota, hand-lettered a huge poster saying "SAVE SHAD-MOOR!" Huge! Visible from the air. Then we discovered that Sunday was also Field Day, an event dedicated to fun and games for the local youth. I said to myself, "Oh my God, maybe nobody will show up."

I remember going up at 11:30 and very few of us were walking up there. Then, at around 11:45 I saw people coming up the path

from Ditch Plains, and then I turned around and saw people coming up from town. I saw families, people who had been at Field
Day left and came there. Airplanes came by, News 12 came by. By
12:10 we had at least 300 people. It was really an amazing day!
The town had people there who saw what we wanted to do. I
think that really turned the corner on Shadmoor.

When asked what message Akin derived from the experience, he
responded,

When people really want to get something done, and it's the right
thing, you can find a way to do it. We did this in seven days. From
that point on, the town said: We've got to save this property.

A few days later, Akin and more than two dozen others from the town
went to Riverhead to speak to the County Legislature on behalf of funding for Shadmoor. "The idea of Shadmoor becoming four lots for four
millionaires is unacceptable," he told them. The Nature Conservancy's
Stuart Lowrie also urged the Legislature to support a bond authorization for the purchase of Shadmoor. Legislator Guldi had been lobbying
his fellow lawmakers all day on that Tuesday. Late that night, he and
Michael Caracciola, a co-sponsor of a bill to obtain the County Executive's "certificate of necessity," won its approval. "It was a big day,"
Guldi said. He claimed that Robert Gaffney, the County Executive, and
his staff "went above and beyond, in terms of the effort."

In the November 1999 election Jay Schneiderman defeated Cathy
Lester for East Hampton Town Supervisor. Lester, a Democrat, had for
years been a major champion for the save Shadmoor cause and many
locals thought her loss meant that any chance for saving the property
was gone. Fortunately Schneiderman picked up right where Lester had
left off and, along with the GSF and TNC, pushed hard at both the
county and state levels to build a coalition to buy Shadmoor. One
recurring problem was that the appraised value of the property kept
falling short of the asking price. Land prices had begun to appreciate so
fast that by the time each new appraisal was finished, the price had
gone up. Nevertheless Schneiderman, with major help from Stuart
Lowrie of The Nature Conservancy, was able to keep the Town and the

A 20-year struggle ends with a new state park.

county committed, but there was a problem getting the state to commit. Apparently the state matching funds were tied up in Albany politics. According to both Schneiderman and Assemblyman Fred Thiele, it was at this point that Perry Duryea made a call to Albany that broke the logjam. The state was finally onboard. One year after the rally, the negotiations for Shadmoor were consummated. WE DID IT! SHADMOOR IS SAVED headlined the CCOM newsletter. The price for the purchase was $17,500,000. The breakdown of the contributions worked out to $5.5 million dollars from the Town ($3 million coming from the Community Preservation Fund), $5.6 million from New York state, $5.4 million from Suffolk County, and $1 million from The Nature Conservancy, which brokered the deal.

Larry Penny calls the acquisition of Shadmoor a turning point. Recalling that the Sanctuary property was also lined up for development, he believes that "if they [the developers] had gotten Shadmoor through, they would have gotten these other things through. Shadmoor was kind of the Armageddon."

Not everyone shared this viewpoint on the Shadmoor acquisition. Russell Stein expressed his disappointment in the way it went:

I love it [Shadmoor]. What makes me angry about Shadmoor is how long it went on and the money that was spent when we have spineless politicians who could have put the whole thing away for a million dollars.

When questioned why that didn't happen, Stein commented that in the 1980s the Planning Board was extremely weak:

We had mandatory cluster legislation and they didn't use it. It was a perfect place to use it.

When the *East Hampton Star* ran a story about the saving of Shadmoor, it noted that "State Assemblyman Fred Thiele praised CCOM for its unwavering fight to get the property preserved. They are an example of a public citizenry who knows what they want and are willing to fight for it, and they've done an outstanding job."

On October 26, 2000, government dignitaries and representatives of the several environmental organizations that had worked long and diligently for its acquisition gathered at the site near a handsome new sign that read, "Welcome to Shadmoor State Park." The sign notes that the property is owned in partnership with Suffolk County, the Town of East Hampton, and The Nature Conservancy, and is managed by the Town of East Hampton. A 20-year struggle had ended in victory.

Culloden Point

Culloden Point, 272 magnificent acres of open land in Montauk, features over a mile of waterfront overlooking Fort Pond Bay. The property was named for the H.M.S. Culloden, a 74-gun British ship that went aground at that point in 1781. It also has more archeological significance than any other location in town, being particularly rich in Indian artifacts. But like other open spaces in Montauk, Culloden came into the sights of developers in the mad rush to build in the 1980s. The owner of the property, 511 Equities Corporation, and its principal, Lawrence Liebman of New York, had applied to subdivide the parcel, located between Flamingo Avenue and Block Island Sound, into 77 house lots.

In CCOM's files appears an unusual memorandum dated August 1, 1989. The author is "NNK" (presumably Nancy Nagle Kelley), and the memo is addressed to "Mike and Steve" (Bottini and Biasetti of the Group for the South Fork, respectively). It is instructive as a model of organizational strategy at work:

1. Think up group name and slogan. Get individuals and groups to sign onto letterhead: GSF, CCOM, Natural History Society, TNC, Culloden Point Association, Suffolk Archaeological Association, noteworthy individuals.

2. Prepare a fact sheet and map on Culloden similar to ones for Hither Woods and Barcelona Neck [in East Hampton].

3. Review Impact Statement and articulate what resources will be lost due to development.

4. Generate general publicity about need to preserve Culloden; community education.

   A. Have people write letters to Editor

   B. Bumper stickers

5. Presentation to Planning Board and Town Board on value of Culloden Point:

   Slide show

   1 page fact sheet

   Get a crowd there

6. Slide show—use: aerial photos, archaeological features, scenic vistas, trails, water views, vegetation, wetlands onsite.

   Put together narrative for show based on fact sheet.

7. Begin letter campaign to Town, county, and state officials to get their support for preservation.

8. Review EQBA [Environmental Quality Bond Act] applications for Hither Woods and Barcelona Neck. Begin collecting similar information for Culloden.

9. Find out what information DEC already has on Culloden.

10. Contact archaeological expert to determine Culloden's significance.

12. Get letters of support from regional, national environmental groups.

Just west of the highly developed Montauk Harbor area, the Culloden Point Preserve (below) and North Neck Preserve (above) create a greenbelt from Block Island Sound to Lake Montauk.

Following these guidelines, an intensive campaign got underway by a new coalition of which CCOM was key, the Culloden Point Alliance. At the Town level, Larry Penny credits Lisa Liquori of the Planning Department and then-Supervisor Cathy Lester for their efforts in pushing for acquisition. Some six years later, in 1995, after negotiations on many fronts, 192 acres of the total 272 acres finally went into preserve status. CCOM actively participated in urging all governmental agencies to save the entire parcel because of the lack of sufficient public water and erosion of the bluffs, as well as Culloden's fragile wetlands.

CCOM's files show copies of correspondence from the Trust for Public Land (TPL), a land conservation organization specializing in the protection of both urban and rural open spaces, whose mission is to secure lands for eventual transfer to public land management agencies. The letters, dated March 1988, were addressed to Andrew Sabin, an affluent Amagansett resident and an executive board member of The Nature Conservancy. Initially, they describe negotiations with the

Culloden Point tract owners and being in contact with TNC, the Group for the South Fork, the New York Department of Environmental Conservation (DEC), and "local officials." Though they asked Sabin for information, reading between the lines it would appear they were also hoping for financial support.

Eight months after the letter to Sabin, this missive from the TPL was sent to Sara Davison, the executive director of the South Fork/Shelter Island Chapter of The Nature Conservancy:

> It appears that DEC will not be in a position to allocate monies in the short or medium term for the acquisition of Culloden Point. Because of previous priorities for EQBA funds on Long Island, Culloden Point, at a cost of $7.5 to $8 million, will not be a fundable project for this year. The land, and its flora and fauna, are so visually and environmentally significant that we hope The Nature Conservancy will be able to pursue the project.... We notified the owner of the property that our negotiations were at an end.

CCOM's March 1994 newsletter was devoted exclusively to an in-depth description of the four parcels of open acreage that CCOM found imperative for preservation: Culloden Point, Shadmoor, the Sanctuary,

---

CULLODEN

The prominent highlands know as Culloden Point were a favorite of the early Americans, and they left behind a rich legacy there. With what is one of the very few year-round stream of any size in Montauk, it combines water from runoff, seeps, and springs comprising a large watershed of forested slopes, shallow sedgy pans, and swampy water holes scattered over an area of more than 150 acres. On its way to the sea it carries this water for a mile or more, slowly meandering in the shade of fern-covered banks and through silty meadows to empty into Fort Pond Bay.

The Culloden forest is 100% hardwoods, tupelos, red maples, oaks, hickories, beech, and sassafras, many nearly 100 feet high, taller than anywhere else on the South Fork except Gardiner's island.

and the Benson Reservation. Rav Freidel reported at a CCOM executive board meeting in January, 1995, that "the GSF [Group for the South Fork's] position is that total acquisition of the land is unlikely and that the most we can hope for is to reduce a little further the number of homes that can be built." He added Assistant Town Attorney Rick Whalen's opinion that the price tag on Culloden was so high that it would come down to trade-offs—if Culloden were preserved in its entirety, other parcels would not get acquired. Therefore, Culloden's high price tag and the possibility of trade-offs was a significant consideration. Nevertheless, after discussion of the GSF position, the CCOM board decided to push for total acquisition anyway, with the philosophy that open space once lost is lost forever.

A state grant of $1 million had been promised, which the Town would be required to match. County Legislator Fred Thiele had introduced legislation to get the county to contribute. In a letter to him in May of 1990, CCOM President Carol Morrison wrote

> ...we are deeply grateful for your strong support of the preservation of Culloden. It is such a distinctive tract of land and waterfront combined. Its preservation as open space would give so much benefit to the public both because of its unique environmental quality as well as its beauty. Your introduction to the County Legislature of a bill to secure $1.7 million from the county toward purchasing this property brings us that much closer to making its acquisition a reality. Now we must go to work to get the Environmental Bond Act of 1990 passed. We will certainly do everything we can to accomplish this since these funds could very readily make up the difference in what is needed for acquisition...

The 21st Century Environmental Bond Act of 1990 mentioned in the letter was actively supported by CCOM, in the hope it would provide matching funds for the acquisition of Culloden and other open space. But while Long Island voters went for it, voters upstate defeated it. As a consequence, there would be no funding for land acquisition by the Department of Environmental Conservation.

In July of 1991, President Carol Morrison wrote to Kevin Law, the Director of Suffolk County's Real Estate Division, that "the county has already recognized the importance for acquisition with a commitment of $1.7 million to be funded from the open space program. The state, too, has recognized its importance by assigning a matching grant of $1.0 million for its acquisition. East Hampton has met this challenge." The response was a disappointment: "Although the property at Culloden Point is environmentally sensitive land, the county does not have the funding, at the present time, to pursue this parcel," Law's office wrote back.

The monies raised were inadequate to cover the hefty price tag of $11 million to save the whole parcel. However, in 1996, an amazing 71% of East Hampton voters approved passage of a $5 million Town bond. "CCOM was proud to be a part of an East End coalition that created brochures, passed out flyers, and placed radio ads to ensure that voters knew the details of the propositions and the importance of their passage," reported the November 1996 Newsletter. Six million dollars of Supervisor Cathy Lester's new capital budget called for open space acquisition in 1997, including Culloden Point.

"The big thing was the developers were moving ahead and we were having a hard time trying to get the money to save it," Carol Morrison recalls. "It finally came up that the people who were developing it discovered it was the old town dump... so that gave it a bad name.... it had a slope to it and you couldn't build on a slope. Little by little we saved as much as 63% of it."

Not everyone was content with that 63 percent. "I would have liked to have gotten the whole thing," laments Larry Penny. "The Town chose the Sanctuary over Culloden." But Bill Akin thinks that overall, "it worked out well; we got 192 acres preserved."

Amsterdam Beach

Amsterdam Beach, the last large undeveloped oceanside property (123 acres), came up for subdivision approval in 2002, prompting CCOM to push for acquisition. Lying just across from Theodore Roosevelt County Park and running from Route 27 to the ocean, it is adjacent to the Montauk Association Houses and the Andy Warhol Preserve (owned by The Nature Conservancy). It is comprised of small ponds

From the small pond (right foreground) back to Rt. 27, Amsterdam Beach is over 100 acres of wetland and virgin marsh land just acquired.

and wetlands and has been described as part of a block of 2,815 acres of high-quality vegetation, of which 2,400 are already protected from future development. This greatly enhances its importance for the integrity of this ecosystem.

In March of 2003, a CCOM board member reported that Congressman Tim Bishop had secured $300,000 to be used toward the purchase of the property. However, he had also heard from Parks Commissioner Bernadette Castro that the budget had been cut. An action alert was sent to CCOM members that summer. "Montauk's Amsterdam Beach is being threatened by development! We want New York State to buy it," the alert said. The missive described the property as the Town's number-one priority for acquisition and also as number one on The Nature Conservancy's list. It ended with an ardent plea for members to write to their appropriate representatives: "Time is of the essence. There is virtually no oceanfront property for sale left on Long Island…. We must save Amsterdam Beach!"

Pristine Amsterdam Beach fronts on the Atlantic Ocean and stretches back to Rt. 27 covering 122 acres.

In August, Rav Freidel accompanied assemblyman Fred Thiele and representatives from the Town and state parks, the office of Senator Ken Lavalle, The Nature Conservancy, and the Community Preservation Fund Committee on a walk-through of the property to reinforce the importance of securing funding for this significant parcel.

Following the 2003 burst of activity, news about Amsterdam Beach dropped off suddenly. In the mysterious world of property acquisitions, this can sometimes be a good thing. And so it was with Amsterdam. In June of 2005, *Newsday* reported that a deal had been reached. Then, on July 1, the East Hampton Town Board passed a resolution to acquire the property, with help from the county, state, and even the federal government. Montauk's southern coastline from the lighthouse to Ditch Plains had been saved.

On July 30, 2005, Governor Pataki signed the contract for New York State to join the Town of East Hampton, Suffolk County and the Federal government in the purchase of Amsterdam Beach. Also attending (left to right) Kevin McDonald of The Nature Conservancy, East Hampton Councilman Job Potter, and NY Assemblyman Fred Thiele.

AMSTERDAM

This 122-acre parcel has been completely undisturbed for most of the last century and up until the present. It is comprised of maritime shrub and grassland and contains a remarkable range of habitat, with moorland, freshwater ponds, marshes, meadows, and forest. The vegetation, primarily shadbush, high-bush blueberry, black cherry, and arrowwood, provides extensive habitat for a wide range of bird species, from the northern harrier and Coopers hawk to the huge variety of birds that use the Great Eastern Flyway. The wetlands provide crucial habitat to species such as woodfrogs, toads, eastern ribbon snakes, spring peepers, and spotted and painted turtles. The blue-spotted salamander, a protected species, and the four-toed salamander, have been identified on-site during breeding season.

Montauk is all about contrast. The 19th-century Association Houses designed by McKim, Mead, and White are situated right next door to the highly dense Montauk Shores Condominiums in the Ditch Plains area.

The acquisition of the two Hither Hills properties, Shadmoor, Culloden, and Camp Hero spanned two decades, the 1980s and 1990s, and even carried over into the 21st century. Over that period CCOM had matured into an established and respected environmental organization. Much of what had been accomplished would not have come about had CCOM not strengthened crucial alliances (for example, with the Group for the South Fork) and made new ones (such as with The Nature Conservancy). Many new members and directors rallied to the organization over this stretch of years. Rav Freidel, Richard Kahn, Larry Smith, Ed Porco, and Lisa Grenci, among others, joined the loyal "old-timers" on the front lines at town hall meetings, CCOM-sponsored events, and generally made sure the environmental cause was always clearly on the radar screen.

While open space battles had occupied much of CCOM's energy, the accelerating pace of development forced other issues upon the organization. Protecting Montauk's groundwater, attempting to reverse years of neglect for Lake Montauk, and postponing the development rush by derailing the idea of extending a superhighway to Montauk were some. All these issues and more fell to the active members of CCOM. And while some people still hold CCOM responsible for the huge traffic nightmare facing the East End today, it is doubtful whether any of the preserved open space acquired in the 80's and 90's would have been saved if the Sunrise Highway ended in Montauk or even Amagansett. "It would have been convenient to have the highway," Bill Akin says, "but... there's a point where inconvenience doesn't enter into the equation. It takes a bit of work to get out here, but it's a small price to pay."

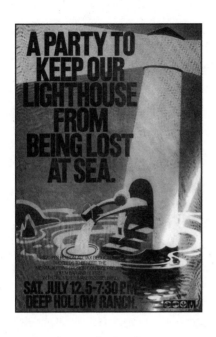

Chapter 3

Other Land Issues

HILE THE MAJOR BATTLES TO PRESERVE the open spaces of Shadmoor, Hither Woods, Camp Hero, and Culloden Point were among CCOM's primary concerns, there were many other important land preservation issues that the organization took up from the 1970s through the 1990s. The drive to develop Montauk did not abate during these decades; it was a constant battle for those concerned with the environment. Without the efforts of CCOM, Montauk would undoubtedly have succumbed to overdevelopment. Saving land is saving wilderness, and it is also deciding how to use it best for the residents who enjoy it. These are some of the other significant land issues that were integral to Montauk's unique character.

Halt the Highway

MONTAUK IS THE END OF THE LINE... WILL THE HIGHWAY BE THE END OF MONTAUK? asked a punchy advertisement in the September 12, 1974 *East Hampton Star*. CCOM board member James Procter, a theatrical publicity agent, has been credited with many of the creative publicity concepts used by the organization. The ad invited citizens to the Montauk Fire House to hear the pros and cons of the proposed Sunrise Highway extension (which would bypass the local towns). Dr. Ian Marceau, director of the Group for America's South Fork, was to report on how several issues of concern "will affect you, your property, and your business."

The plans for the Sunrise extension were initiated in 1969 through then-Governor Hugh Carey's application to the federal government for funding (although he later stated his opposition to it in January of 1975). In November of 1969 he appointed a South Fork Transportation Task force. Hilda Lindley wrote a letter to Carey pointing out that the Task Force was in the hands of pro-extension people, and that Halt the Highway protest leaders Tom Twomey and Charles and Audrey Raebeck were excluded. Judith Hope, who ran successfully for Town Council in 1973, had this to say regarding the unbalanced political scene during that period: "I found Suffolk County politics extremely corrupt.... I resented, especially, the one-party manipulation of candidates and legislation here extending right into Albany through Perry Duryea and his man on the scene, Henry Mund." Mund was East Hampton councilman as well as executive assistant to assembly speaker Duryea.

CCOM was a key force in support of the Halt the Highway group. Secretary Kay Dayton was named to the Halt the Highway executive committee and CCOM Vice President Hal B. Lary was a member of the advisory board of the organization. In keeping with Hilda Lindley's strong, positive views on the importance and effectiveness of coalitions, CCOM was part of the sponsoring umbrella group, the East End Council of Organizations. The Southampton Council of Community Organizations was also part of the umbrella group. With support from both East Hampton Town Councilwoman Judith Hope and Southampton Supervisor Theodore Hulse, the group undertook an intensive postcard and telephone campaign to convince people that extending the highway to create a bypass would result in a population explosion on the South Fork with its attendant congestion and taxes for infrastructure. Not everyone was opposed to the extension of the highway; many local business owners, in fact, were for it. A more accessible highway would bring more people and thus more business. One of the proponents of the extension was local son Perry Duryea.[1]

On April 20, 1974, CCOM presented four speakers at a public meeting on the issue of halting further development of the Sunrise Highway Extension and promoting instead improvement of the Long Island Railroad service to Montauk. At the meeting, Tom Downey, Democratic legislator from Islip, offered to introduce a resolution putting the county on record in opposition to the highway extension. Tom Twomey, the head of the Halt the Highway Committee, announced that the Southampton, North Haven, Quogue, and Westhampton Beach Town Boards had voted resolutions objecting to the extension of the highway. The committee was seeking unanimous support from the Town Board of East Hampton.

Also present at the public meeting was Ron Ziel, a railway historian, who told of some serious problems with the condition of the Long Island Railroad roadbed, the inadequate amounts of money that had been allocated by the state, and the positive features of railroad use in comparison with other transportation. Ron Kane, a representative of the Metropolitan Transportation Authority, emphasized the fact that the railroad had no money, as the New York State Legislature had failed to come through with an announced allocation of $50 million. "Money is the crucial factor in determining the future of the railroad," he said.

Twomey's letter to supporters of the Halt the Highway project was encouraging to those who had anticipated further battles to preserve the relative solitude of Montauk.

April, 1975

Dear Friend,

As you have probably heard, Governor Carey has withdrawn the New York State application to the Federal Highway Administration for location approval of the Sunrise Extension. This action

---

1. "Perry Duryea once was one of the most powerful Republicans in the state," acknowledged a *New York Times* article in 2003, and "was instrumental in the building of the Long Island Expressway and the Sunrise Highway, and also lobbied unsuccessfully to build a highway through the Hamptons to Montauk."

effectively kills the proposed highway since location approval is required in order to secure federal funds for the project....

It is our hope to develop with your help alternative solutions to the traffic problem....

This experience has been particularly rewarding since it clearly proves that when enough citizens feel strongly about an issue, and they are willing to voice publicly their opinion, and work diligently toward their goal, they *can* successfully fight "City Hall."

Though the Halt the Highway drive was successful, it's an issue that never really goes away. It's a natural reaction, whenever someone is stuck in a half-mile jam on a one-time obscure back road, to vent frustration on someone. "If only those bastards had let them build a highway I'd be sipping my merlot by now. What did they accomplish? We got the development anyway." In his song "The Boxer," local Montauk songwriter Paul Simon sings "a man sees what he wants to see and disregards the rest." Those who think the development happened even without the bypass are seeing the buildings; they are not seeing what's been saved. And if a highway had gone through, the development pressure would have been so great that no one could have mounted a coalition to preserve Camp Hero, Hither Hills, Shadmoor, Culloden, and more. Montauk alone would have had at least 1,000 more homes by the year 2000.

Motel Menace

When development pressure increased in the 1980s, proliferating motels became a key concern of CCOM's. An emblematic fight was the Beachcomber Motel. "That was outrageous!" remarks an indignant Carol Morrison. "Originally it was a very attractive, low-key place, and it was bought up by a big developer. First [they] started small, [wanting] only 49 units, being [that] 49 units weren't subject to the State Environmental Quality Review Act (SEQRA). Then the next thing they decided [was] to do another 49, and they did it incrementally, until the last one [of 28 units] and we suddenly realized what they were doing."

The situation was a direct result of smoldering Town politics. In 1982, re-elected Supervisor Mary Fallon, a Republican, had fired the planning department and its director, Tom Thorsen, and instead hired a private pro-development company, Rochris, as consultants to the Town on planning issues. Thorsen, who had been the author of the Town farmland study in 1981, "was very good and forward-looking," according to former Assistant Town Attorney Rick Whalen. "To abolish the planning department was obviously a move to disembowel the environmental protection movement." Thus began what Whalen, Larry Penny, and Russell Stein refer to as "the reign of terror." A developer, quoted by Dan Rattiner in the *Montauk Pioneer*, called it by another name: "This is the East Hampton Town Republican Administration Memorial Building Boom."

Though he believed Supervisor Mary Fallon to have "previously been an environmentalist," Larry Penny states that "the Republican party had been overtaken by what I thought was a bunch of thugs" who wanted to subdivide everything in sight. The reign of terror persisted until 1986, even after there was a change in government and Democrat Judith Hope replaced Fallon as supervisor in 1984. "They [developers] had momentum, especially [regarding] the condos. Those were the four worst years for the environment." Penny turned to the use of wetlands laws to try and stem the tide.

CCOM and others felt that Supervisor Fallon had "political obligations" to the large-scale developers who had supported her re-election campaign in 1981. The Save Our Heritage Committee (later renamed the Citizens Planning Committee), with whom CCOM worked, gathered 1,800 names on a petition urging the Town Board to keep Thorsen as director, and presented it at a public meeting on January 30, 1982. Over 388 people showed up after a flyer flooded the area with this eye-catching headline and text:

BONACKERS & RESIDENTS—ARE YOU STUPID?
That's what the Town Board thinks—they are trying to double-cross us, and they hope we won't notice!

The flyer went on to indict the administration for the firing of Thorsen and the Planning Department, which had been free of political influence. The *East Hampton Star* also printed a letter from a clearly incensed CCOM President Richard Johnson:

> The Board of Directors of CCOM continues to be concerned about the politicalization of East Hampton's planning activities... It now seems that our supervisor is making yet another effort to help developers circumvent the planning process by having Rochris take over the functions of the Planning Department... Any loss of a "watchful eye" on developers will be a tragic loss for Montauk, where East Hampton's greatest potential for future development lies... CCOM urges all taxpayers in East Hampton to rise up on a non-partisan, non-political basis to protest this latest move by Supervisor Fallon to make fools of us all. Let our solidarity force her to reconsider who, in fact, she is working for.

Former Town Councilman Tom Ruhle recalls that no one had done a full review of the Beachcomber Motel because "it was only a 10-unit thing... the Planning Board never looked at the big picture. [The developers] pieced it together. I think it was intentionally overlooked." Moreover, according to Ruhle, in 1982 the Planning Board would go into executive session with the developer and keep the public out. And so, Ruhle says, "John McGowan, the attorney for the developer, EFS Ventures, went into executive session behind closed doors and cut a deal with the Planning Board for more units... those were some of the odd things going on."

Says Carol Morrison, "When they put out that last one [set of 10 units] was when we got angry. One of our biggest complaints was about fire." There was a narrow road potentially impeding fire truck access. Morrison continues:

> We asked for 10 units to be taken down. They [Rochris] went ahead and approved it. For that, we sued. We won that suit. But on appeal they only had to remove four units because the statute of limitations had expired. While only four units came down, the Beachcomber was closed for several years before they got their C.O., and that sent a message to developers who wanted to segment their building applications. Namely, it'll cost you. CCOM is watching.

As Russell Stein recalls,

> During the initial Beachcomber lawsuit I was writing the stuff with
> John Shea. I remember going to Suffolk Supreme Court and going
> head to head with [George] Stankevitch... he was taking all these
> mom-and-pop motels and blowing them up and making condos.
> We had never seen an application form like his. You could read it
> and not know the slightest thing about what this motel really was.

Stein wistfully remembers those earlier buildings, as well.

> They were wonderful. You still see remnants of them along the old
> highway... it turns out most of the motels out there were created by
> Swedish socialists in the middle of the century, like the Umbrella
> Inn, where I stayed. They were interesting people. And Beach-
> comber Inn was four little red-roofed buildings. And they [devel-
> opers] came in and just blew it up... They had maximum density.
> It looks like a jail. They came in under the zoning; at that time there
> were no density limits... The fact was, there was this machine, and
> certain people came in... and they got what they wanted.

A TIDE OF MOTEL PLANS, heralded a *Newsday* headline of December 3,
1983, focusing on East Hampton. Reprinted in the December CCOM
newsletter, the article quoted William Gaylord, vice president of the
Long Island Association of Commerce and Industry, who said, "I can
see that 700 [motel] units (the increase for all of East Hampton)... might
have a significant impact on what the residents see as the quality of
life." Another quote was by Lee Koppelman, executive director of the
Long Island Regional Planning Board. "Certainly there's a legitimate
case for motels, but one of the phenomena taking place is the phony
use of motels—using motels as a backdoor way to build condominiums, which are more lucrative than motels for developers."

A 1984 CCOM newsletter listed the new accommodations in downtown Montauk alone:

> South Euclid apartments, with 8 units; Surf Club, with 92 units;
> Sunscape, with 8 units; Royal Atlantic East, with 38 units; Royal
> Atlantic North, with 39 units; the Tower, with 20 units; Albatross,

The Beachcomber Motel was built in phases to avoid review by the Zoning Board.

plus 6 units; Atlantic Properties, with 7 units; Apartments over John's Drive In, with approx. 2 units; Sea Watch, with 20 units; Sands East, with 7 units; The Dunes, with 23 units. The total: an incredible addition of 270 units with an increase of 405 cars. (This does not include the Montauk Manor's 140 condo units.)

A month later CCOM was actively supporting building moratoria for 180 days, which the new government, now with a Democratic majority, enacted as soon as they took office (in 1984), much to the consternation of developers and the building trades. CCOM noted that there were currently 97 applications under review by the Planning Board, and that 1,942 residential units could be approved in Montauk alone within the year. They identified the additional potential units from those previously cited:

Amsterdam Beach, with 16 units; Windswept, with 12 units; Beachcomber, with 92 units; Fort Pond Realty, with 37 units; Harbor Ridge (Golf Villas), with 24 units; Holiday Acres, with 36 units; Lands End Motel, with 11 units; Offshore Sports Marina, with 42 units; Pine Meadows Motel, with 10 units; Ocean Shores Motel, with 36 units; Star Island Yacht Club, with 42 units. The total? 358 units added to the 1,942 potential residential units.

An added touch of reality was that the Montauk Fire Department placed an urgent ad in the *Star* pleading for new members for their ambulance squad, as they were experiencing a shortage of trained medical personnel due to the increased needs caused by a rapidly growing community. That concern alone tells the story of the consequence of unbridled development to the infrastructure of the community.

CCOM's case against the Town Planning Board in the handling of the Beachcomber was won in the two lower New York courts in Brooklyn. The win was based on the Beachcomber's many irregularities, including the lack of an Environmental Impact Statement.

Sanctuary

As for the acquisition of the Sanctuary property—mentioned by Larry Penny as the trade-off when the Culloden Point deal was in play—it, too, had long been on the CCOM wish list, as well as that of The Nature Conservancy. During the early 1990s CCOM embarked on a campaign to save the last 1,000 acres. CCOM board members identified every vacant parcel of land in Montauk slated for development. Mike Bottini of the Group for the South Fork compiled the data onto a map. The CCOM newsletter spelled out what needed to be done and included Penny's descriptions of the Sanctuary's 310 acres as "thickly vegetated as most rain forests. Its surface is wetter than dry…. It defies traversing." The area consists of almost 70% wetlands, and is a prime habitat for blue-spotted salamanders and other rare species.

In 1982, the Town Planning Board permitted roads to be built without requiring DEIS permits on the Sanctuary land for test hole drilling by the developer who planned to build 144 condominium units. Yet the area had been described by the DEC as "one of the finest examples of freshwater wetlands on all of Long Island." Moreover, an earlier study paid for by the Town established the property as having critical wetlands requiring protection. Montauk Moorlands

Association hired Inter-Science Research to again study the area, this time not overlooking details such as major streams flowing through the property to Oyster Pond.

Assemblyman John Behan wrote to Joan Davidson, New York State Parks and Recreation Commissioner, asking that the land be acquired, as did CCOM President Rav Freidel. Just in time for the organization's annual celebration of Earth Day in April 1997, it was announced that New York State had purchased the 310 acres. "CCOM lobbied for that for a long time," Bill Akin recalls. "The purchase is one of the first projects to receive funding from the Clean Water Clean Air Bond Act," CCOM's newsletter reported. Only passive use would be allowed on the land (such as walking and bird-watching), while motorized vehicles would be disallowed.

Larry Penny offers an offbeat bit of local lore regarding the Sanctuary:

> The Mob was pretty heavily infiltrated in Montauk land. Ultimately, some of them got busted in New York City by the F.B.I.—those involved in the Sanctuary. We never knew their names, but the F.B.I. came for my records, [those of] the Natural Resources Department, the Planning Department—any agency that had the Sanctuary records. Apparently... some of the money was laundered—"Family" money. I was out there one day surveying the wetlands, meeting the surveyor there, when one of the owners pulled up in a big black car with dark windows you couldn't see in. There was a floozie; an attractive-looking young woman in high heels got out. She took one look at the Sanctuary and got back in the car. The owner didn't go [into the woods] either. He smoked a cigar, asked a few questions and drove away.

Penny believes that that was the last attempt to have all the wetlands surveyed in the Sanctuary. It seems the developers were dragging their feet thinking the politics would eventually change and "they'd get to do whatever they wanted," Penny says. "After they were taken to court in New York City, the state stepped in a few years later and bought the whole place." The Nature Conservancy was instrumental in this acquisition.

Pataki: Montauk Buy a Rare Jewel

By Bill Bleyer
STAFF WRITER

Gov. George Pataki marked Earth Day on Long Island yesterday by announcing the state would buy the largest private parcel of land at Montauk Point, bringing the state's holdings there to 1,500 acres.

Surrounded by public officials and environmentalists on the shore of Belmont Lake at the state park of the same name in North Babylon, Pataki said he was pleased to mark the 27th anniversary of Earth Day by detailing plans for the acquisition of a 340-acre Montauk site known locally as "The Sanctuary."

"This is a wonderful piece of land," Pataki said before helping to plant a white oak tree to mark Earth Day. "It is environmentally sensitive. Seventy percent is fresh water wetlands."

To facilitate the acquisition, The Nature Conservancy purchased the property yesterday for $4.18 million from ICR of Montauk, a development company that has tried unsuccessfully to develop it several times. On Tuesday the state plans to buy the site, for the same price, with some of the first money earmarked from the Clean Water / Clean Air Bond Act approved by voters in November.

The land will be owned and managed by the state Office of Parks, Recreation and Historic Preservation. The agency already owns two adjacent sites to the east: the more than 400-acre Camp Hero, a former air defense base, and the 724 acres of Montauk Point State Park.

Al Caccese, deputy park commissioner for land management, said the triangular property, bordered by Montauk Highway and Old Montauk Highway on the north and south, would probably be merged into Montauk Point State Park. "Seventy percent of the property is wetlands so it wouldn't make as much sense to be a self-standing park. There are some great vistas and we anticipate some public use," he said.

Sara Davidson, the Conservancy's Long Island director, said that "because of the environmental sensitivity, the property should be managed as a nature preserve for passive recreation. It's really an extraordinary property. There's great opportunity for hikes and bird watching."

She credited Pataki and state Parks Commissioner Bernadette Castro for their leadership in acquiring "a major jewel in the crown of New York and Long Island's park system."

"We're confident with this purchase we'll be able to preserve . . . many species of birds and water fowl for the next generation and for the next century," Pataki said. There are a number of rare species on the property, including the blue spotted salamander, the spotted turtle and the tall thistle.

Pataki, who recalled coming to Montauk for summer vacations with his wife and children, said the state would be doing more in the future to protect the pine barrens, Long Island Sound and air and water quality.

Buying More Montauk
The 340-acre parcel the state plans to buy at Montauk:

Montauk County Park
Lake Munchogue
Montauk Point State Park
Lake Montauk
Old Montauk Highway
Montauk Point Lighthouse
Camp Hero State Park
Land state will buy
0   MILES   3

NEWSDAY, WEDNESDAY, APRIL 23, 1997

Newsday/Richard Cornett

Newsday Photo: John R. Cornell Jr.
A view inside "The Sanctuary," made up largely of fresh water wetlands.

The state was instrumental in saving the "Sanctuary."
(*Newsday*, April 23, 1997)

THE SANCTUARY

As thickly vegetated as most rain forests, the Sanctuary's 310 acres are replete with wetlands. So dense that it's nearly impenetrable, this is a place where woodcocks hug the ground, trout lily and seorse sedge can be found. Among the forest canopy of oak, swamp maple, black gum, American beech and black birch and understory of shadbush, American holly, gray birches, witch hazel, alternate-leafed dogwood, and mountain laurel are some very large and old specimens of each. The blue-spotted salamander breeds alongside the four-toed salamander and the eastern newt, while spotted, painted, box, and snapping turtles abound.

The Benson Reservation

One of the stranger legal tussles over land in Montauk involved developer Nicola Biase of Montauk Sunbeach II. When Biase purchased a section of Hither Woods from Curtiss–Wright in 1982, the 43 acres of oceanfront land on the Old Montauk Highway was a no-cost throw-in. This property of open oceanfront, the "gateway" to Montauk on Old Montauk Highway, is known as the Hither Plain and Benson Bathing Reservations.

BIASE BUILDS BARRIER, headlined the *East Hampton Star* edition on July 26, 1984, noting that

> a drama was played out on the Montauk oceanfront over the past week, combining plot elements characteristic of the confrontations on the East Hampton Town Stage—history, beach access, property rights, deeds, planning, and the motel business and featuring an increasingly prominent landowner as the central character.... The action began... when motel operators and residents along the Old Montauk Highway and in the Hither Hills subdivision, suddenly found access to the ocean via nine footpaths blocked off with chicken wire, mounds of dirt and "private property" signs. They ran through footpaths known as the Benson Reservation and were long used as public access to the ocean.... The populace were shocked with Biase's assertion that it was his right to blockade as he owned the property.... It was widely believed that this was an act of revenge or to gain leverage with the Town because of the way it has dealt with him.

Tom Ruhle says that he had a direct involvement with much of this situation. "I was partially responsible for the fence going up," he says. "Biase had hired a security force to guard the property. Louise Nielsen had called my father and told us about it. I went down there and tried to get arrested. The security guard went up to Biase, who was sitting in his Porsche, and came back and said, 'Mr. Biase declines to have you arrested.' So this little girl came up and said, 'Can I walk down the path?' I said, 'Sure.'"

According to the *Star* article, Ruhle, who was a Town Planning Board member at the time, jumped over one of the barriers to assert the public's access rights. It also mentioned that Russell Stein, the Town Attorney, called the police that night and told them not to arrest anyone for trespassing until the legal question of whether the public had a right to use the property was resolved. Ruhle says, "The next day they put the [chain-link] fence up. Biase flipped out that the [Town] police wouldn't come, so he called the State Police... Then he hired his security police and put the fence up. No one knows who cut the fence down. Biase swears it was me."

Biase's blocking of access to the 43 acres resulted in a lawsuit brought privately by a group of residents with property directly across from the ocean, who feared Sunbeach would build houses in the reservation. The litigants were Madge Schneiderman (mother of the current County Legislator and 2000–2004 East Hampton Town Supervisor) and her motel, the Breakers; the Atlantic Bluffs Club (a co-op of 56 apartments); Alfred F. and Louise Nielsen, owners of Twin Pond Motel; William Bruder; and George and Margaret B. Potts. John Shea of Twomey, Latham, Shea, and Kelley was hired and the lawsuit initiated in March of 1985.

The case was of particular interest to the community, as it traced the historical perspective of Montauk land from the ascension of Wyandanch, sovereign of the Montauks, through the East Hampton Proprietors of Montauk[2] to the heirs of Arthur Benson, and the covenants and restrictions regarding the common use of the "Reservations." Those whose property derives from the Benson heirs included an estimated 800 to 1,200 deed holders in Montauk.

Carol Morrison explains that the owner of the Breakers Motel, Madge Schneiderman, whom she described as "a real fighter," initially brought the suit against Biase. At that point CCOM could not

---

2. Individual East Hampton men and Trustees of East Hampton Town bought all of Montauk in 1687, having been authorized by the Dongen Patent of 1686. These men were called the Proprietors. The original Proprietors were Thomas Baker, Robert Bond, Thomas James, Lion Gardiner, John Mulford, and Benjamin Price. In 1754 the Indians and Proprietors made an agreement permitting the Indians to live in Montauk under certain conditions. There followed much disagreement among the heirs of these men and many legal suits followed later.

The inland parcel known as "The Sanctuary" is located between Rt. 27 and Old Montauk Highway. Grazing pastures and the open fields of Theodore Roosevelt County Park are also shown.

legally participate, as this was a private citizen's suit. "The Potts family and Louise Nielsen were involved because they had deeds that said they had a right of way on that property, and that the property was a reservation. So initially in order to help, CCOM provided money for research, with some members going to the Brooklyn Library to look up Arthur Benson for background information to shed light on the situation."

Between 1985 and 1991, while the lawsuit was still pending, there were unsuccessful attempts to negotiate with Mr. Biase. Then, in 1991, through the intercession of The Nature Conservancy, the county offered to buy Biase out. But the sale could not go through with a pending lawsuit, and all the litigants had to agree to the terms of the sale. Only the Breakers motel and the Atlantic Bluffs Club were paying the legal costs at that point. The Atlantic Bluffs Club was mostly in favor of the county purchase, but the Breakers was opposed for a number of reasons. The deal fell through.

The case continued until finally, in 1994, the litigants won a major victory. State Supreme Court Justice William Underwood ruled that

Biase/Sunbeach did not have the right to block access paths to the Benson Reservation. "He based his decision on the original subdivision of Montauk by developer Arthur Benson, who wanted to give everyone who bought property the right to go to the ocean, and to use the woods near it for recreation," reported a March 9, 1994, *New York Newsday* article.

Euphoria among the litigants was short-lived, however. Biase and Sunbeach indicated that they would appeal the decision.

Even before this point, the Breakers, disagreeing with John Shea's legal approach, had decided to go their own way. They hired their own lawyer, and separate papers were filed, escalating the legal costs. (Close to $200,000 was spent by the Atlantic Bluffs Club over the course of the suit, while the Breakers claimed to have spent $150,000.) According to Céline Keating, a CCOM board member who was also on the board of the Atlantic Bluffs Club and who served as legal liaison from the Bluffs Club to attorney Shea, it is widely held that it was Shea's work that won the lawsuit. So at the point when the suit was won, the Atlantic Bluffs Club was essentially carrying the case alone.

Given Biase's appeal of the decision, and the prospect of even more expense, the co-op owners and board at Atlantic Bluffs Club balked. Many owners, not wanting to pay any more legal assessments, wanted to drop the suit and try instead to seek a deal with Biase. But Keating and others felt that the entire reservation should be retained as open space and were opposed to any negotiation with Biase that wouldn't safeguard this. Keating brought her concerns to the CCOM board.

The situation for CCOM was a tricky one. Although the suit was brought privately, its success would nevertheless benefit all of Montauk. If the Atlantic Bluffs Club backed out of the lawsuit, Biase would prevail, and the open space and vistas would be lost. So CCOM devised a plan to raise money through a special appeal that would make it permissible for the organization to help defray the Atlantic Bluff's legal costs.

In a letter to John Taylor, president of the Atlantic Bluffs Club, CCOM President Rav Freidel committed the organization to financially assist in the suit up to $5,000 in a matching grant, which would go to Twomey, Latham, Shea and Kelley, the litigant's attorneys. Freidel cautioned that the motivation for the financial assistance was "to benefit the Montauk community at large" and not just the private interests of the plaintiffs and other owners. Moreover, he said, "CCOM believes it is important that Justice Underwood's decision be affirmed as written and we would not be prepared to assist the Club in this matter if the Club takes any action that might indicate the Club would be satisfied with anything less." (For example, the Atlantic Bluffs Club, the Breakers, any other motel, or any co-op owner could not negotiate separate deals with Biase to allow access for just their owners/renters.) With the promise of help from CCOM, and with additional pledges of contributions from some Bluff's owners, Keating was able to persuade the Atlantic Bluffs Club board not to negotiate with Biase and to continue the legal battle.

The strategy paid off. Three years later, in 1997, the Appellate Division of the State Supreme Court fully affirmed the decision of Judge Underwood. Biase was ordered "to remove any and all fences and structures and restore said Reservations to their original open and natural state, forthwith." The common use of the Benson Reservation was finally upheld. Céline Keating says that this major victory for open space and for the Town would have been lost without CCOM's help.

In a surprise move, in January of 1999 at a ceremony at Gurney's Inn, Biase, the plaintiff of over 10 years of a bitter, expensive lawsuit, signed over title to the Benson Reservations to the Town of East Hampton. Invoking the names of Mary Gosman and Debra Foster, he declared he wanted to honor them for teaching him that land has value beyond price and to appreciate the importance of open space. (Cynics believed that as the land could not be developed, Biase simply decided to settle for a big tax write-off by making the donation.)

Just before the center of Montauk village proper, on the most easterly part of the reservation, stands a boulder with a bronze plaque on it. This part of Montauk history is literally written in stone:

A plaque on a rock just west of Montauk recognizes those who fought to
preserve what is most commonly known as the Benson Reservation.

HITHER PLAIN RESERVATION

THIS NATURE PRESERVE WAS ESTABLISHED BY THE ESTATE OF
ARTHUR W. BENSON ON DECEMBER 12, 1905. THE HITHER PLAIN
RESERVATION WAS ACCEPTED INTO THE EAST HAMPTON TOWN
PARK SYSTEM ON JANUARY 23, 1999, AFTER A LENGTHY BATTLE THAT
SUCCESSFULLY PROTECTED IT FROM PRIVATE DEVELOPMENT.

In Loving Memory of
Madge Schneiderman 1922–1990
Alfred F. Nielsen 1919–1997
George Potts 1914–2000
Who Fought Diligently With Those Listed Below To
Preserve This Property As It Was Originally Intended.
The Atlantic Bluffs Club, The Breakers Motel, Louise Nielsen,
Margaret Potts, And the Concerned Citizens of Montauk.

Fort Hill Cemetery

Until the twentieth century Indians, fish, and cattle dominated Montauk's history. While the herds of cattle succumbed to economic forces and moved west, at least the remains of the Indian civilization lay buried in Montauk's soil. One well-known Indian burial ground occupies a portion of an 11-acre hill overlooking Fort Pond from a bluff directly in front of the gargantuan Montauk Manor Hotel, a relic of the Fisher dream-gone-broke era. The Indians chose well. The bluff is far enough from the ocean to warm up early in spring. It faces southwest into the prevailing summer wind and sun, and the early May shadbush bloom is the most intense on the entire peninsula. And so in May of 1983, on their way to a CCOM executive board meeting, CCOM directors Carol Morrison and Russell Stein were horrified to see unauthorized construction bulldozers working at the important archeological site. "The meeting was adjourned early," Morrison recalls, "so the group could proceed to the Indian site where work was reported to be in progress, illegally."

Larry Penny explains that the survey company Wallbridge, owned by Darrell Weaver and Frank Dragotta, "had a lot of silent partners. They were trying to develop the old Indian burial ground there. They were out there bulldozing. That was going too far... I remember Russell Stein went to court and the Town got an injunction."

Soon after the discovery, CCOM held a public meeting on May 21. Russell Stein moderated, and the speakers were Rick Whalen and Robert Cooper, a Montaukett descendant who later took legal action. New Town Councilman Tony Bullock explained the steps the Town was taking to locate the grave sites and halt development until more knowledge was gained.

The Town Board responded to the public concern regarding the threatened archeological site and hired Edward Johannemann as the archaeologist to study the area. Meanwhile, following up on an idea first conceived by CCOM Director Neil Mahoney, Richard White, Jr. proposed that a Town cemetery be established to preserve the Indian burial grounds as well as provide the people of Montauk with a cemetery. An ad hoc committee to investigate the possibility included

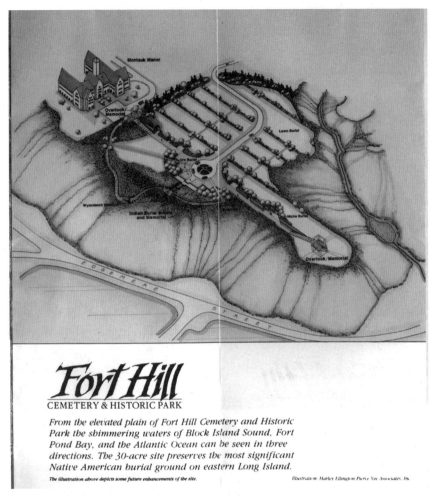

Fort Hill
CEMETERY & HISTORIC PARK

From the elevated plain of Fort Hill Cemetery and Historic Park the shimmering waters of Block Island Sound, Fort Pond Bay, and the Atlantic Ocean can be seen in three directions. The 30-acre site preserves the most significant Native American burial ground on eastern Long Island.

The illustration above depicts some future enhancements of the site.

Illustration: Harley Ellington Pierce Yee Associates, Inc.

Fort Hill Cemetery and Historic Park pamphlet (1994). The cemetery was almost a condo site until CCOM stepped in to block the bulldozers.

Michael Finazzo, Peggy Joyce, William DePouli, and Richard White, who had pledged $250 toward the goal. They hired Joan Hatfield as their attorney. CCOM worked to raise the $3,200 and more in required legal funds, involving the AARP, the Montauk Historical Society, the Montauk Village Association, the Montauk Beach Property Owners Association, the Culloden Shores Association, and individual donors. By November, the Town Board approved funding to buy 30.38 acres for $1.4 million from the Fort Hill and Signal Hill Associates and William Brinkman, Jr.

"James Ketcham, a Montauk lawyer and Fort Hill Cemetery Advisory Committee member, urges the East Hampton Town Board to make the cemetery a municipal one, not one by a public corporation."

However, the start of the following year brought a change in Town government, and an unusual press conference was called in January. The *East Hampton Star* called it "a rare occurrence in local government... with Town officials close-mouthed about its subject." The new supervisor, Judith Hope, announced that "the Town would proceed with condemnation of Fort Hill, rather than the acquisition negotiated by the previous administration."

The decision was based on several "irregularities." The outstanding irregularity was the contracts of sale drawn by the owners' attorney, John McGowan, which omitted the 11 acres of the 30-acre site that had been identified as the Montaukett burial ground. Councilman Bullock and Town Attorney Russell Stein noticed the omission of the 11-acre tract, which Hope deemed "a prime buildable portion of the property." McGowan, who drew up the contract and was also a co-owner, labeled the omission "inadvertent." The *Star*'s report continued, "Democratic members of the Town Board, however, expressed doubts about whether the omission was an honest oversight. Said Hope, 'It is possible that the action I am taking today will save the Town from the biggest land scandal and rip-off of taxpayer's money in the history of the Town.'"

Thoughts of scandal soon dissipated. The Town of East Hampton went ahead and acquired the entire bluff, including the Indian burial site and additional acreage. The non-Indian parcel soon became the Fort Hill Cemetery, where recently departed "Montauk Indians" now rest in peace side by side with their historical soul brothers.

On May 29, 1985, the CCOM newsletter reported that the title to the Fort Hill property—including the Indian burial grounds—had been vested in the Town. The Indian burial grounds were safe.

The Lighthouse Bluffs

"Montauk Point is no longer a point. It's more like a stub," pronounced Coast Guard Petty Officer W. Gene Hughes who, with a tenacious 76-year-old woman, Giorgina Reid, had initiated the fight in the early 1970s to save the Montauk lighthouse, which was endangered by bluff erosion. (Reid was to later author a book on the subject, *How to Hold Up a Bank*.) She and Hughes were invited to address the May 1986 CCOM meeting on the topic of the reed/trench method of stabilization. Reid's concept was to create terraces around the lighthouse, planting reeds to hold the soil.

"Giorgina Reid's was a novel idea: that you could use nature to deal with natural problems, instead of bringing in a bunch of engineers, paving this and reinforcing that," Tom Ruhle says. "And it worked! And, of course, it needed support. It was the first time for something like that."

Carol Morrison remembers Reid as "a little mite of a person. She had started to come out here on her own to try to stop the erosion of the lighthouse area. Her husband who came with her was an artist, and they came from Rocky Point. Every Saturday, no matter what, even in

Pulitzer Prize-winning playwright Edward Albee (at microphone) helps CCOM pick winners at the annual raffle (2003).

Honoring CCOM Supporters: Famed photographer Peter Beard (left) and actress Uta Hagen (right) attend CCOM's summer gala with President Richard Johnson (1974).

the rain, she was there." CCOM provided fundraising money for the project, and volunteers from the organization, along with other people in the community and the Coast Guard, were involved in the work. Morrison proudly recalls that some of her nephews in Westhampton came to help with this singular project.

In reporting on the success of the rainy summer gala of July 1986 to benefit Reid's Montauk Light Erosion Control Project, CCOM's newsletter write-up stated that "even though it rained, people said it was the best ever." Credit was given to chair Kay Carley and many volunteers. "The fishermen gave the buffet a special gourmet treat. Captain John Nolan of the Laurie Dory and Captain David Krusa of the Deliverance donated the fish for Stephanie Krusa's fabulous New England fish chowder. Other fishermen donated a 40-pound smoked sturgeon and bluefish. Also, because of his great interest in preserving the Lighthouse, Richard White, Jr., donated a generous gift of liquor." Playwright Edward Albee bartended at the event, and actors Uta Hagen and Dick Cavett came up with clever presentations for the raffle prizes (one of many July fundraising parties CCOM organized over the years). The gala raised $6,500 toward Reid's lighthouse project. It was a terrific example of the community's response. It took many years and a lot more money before the lighthouse was saved, but CCOM was proud to be the organization to step in as the first financial supporter.

The Land Transfer Tax

During the fight to save Hither Woods, Dan Rattiner, the publisher of the *Montauk Pioneer*, told Rav Freidel that every house built in Hither Woods is one more family that will read his newspaper.

While the wisdom of preserving open space is obvious to CCOM, it takes years, sometimes even decades, to impart that wisdom to both the voters and the politicians. Oak trees don't vote. Osprey don't pay taxes. Fox don't create jobs, and open space costs millions and takes property off the tax rolls.

Fortunately, it has been proven both locally and in other towns around the country that open space is truly the best buy: It has no major infrastructure costs like new roads and maintenance, extra police and fire protection, new water mains and sewage treatment facilities, more schools and teachers, and so on. Open space is one of the prime reasons people come to Montauk. However, the problem is coming up with the money to buy the land.

Money from the federal government is virtually impossible to get because the Town is competing with land in the West, where acres cost hundreds of dollars, not hundreds of thousands of dollars. State and county money is hard to get because there are other, equally deserving properties, and bureaucrats like to spread the money around. And Town politicians are leery of raising taxes and getting voted out of office for not being fiscally responsible.

During the 1980s, as land prices soared and East Hampton found itself getting priced out of the acquisition market by private land buyers, the idea came up to create a land bank to be funded by a small transfer tax placed on the buyer every time land was sold. It was modeled on Rhode Island and Massachusetts legislation and fought for by the Group's Kevin MacDonald and Assemblyman Fred Thiele. (For years environmental groups had tried in vain to get Montauk's own—Assemblyman John Behan—to bring it to the floor of the State Assembly for a vote, but he was unable to do so.)

Finally, in response to explosive development pressures in eastern Suffolk, the transfer tax found new life. Supervisor Cathy Lester's compiled statistics showed that East Hampton Town's housing units had increased a shocking 140% in the 20 years between 1970 and 1990, the largest increase of housing units of any on the East End. The need for additional funds to protect open space and farmland was urgent. In December, 1997, a number of environmental groups throughout the North and South Forks sponsored a day of "East End Rescue Planning Meetings," attended by CCOM members. Experts described different tools for preservation at the meeting. The Proposition idea was developed from that. It was hailed as the most important environmental legislation in decades. It was to add a 2% fee to be paid by the purchaser on improved property worth over $250,000; $100,000 for vacant land. Funds were to be deposited in the East Hampton Community Preservation Fund.

CCOM had pressed members to flood Governor Pataki's office regarding the land-tax bill. In the following spring, many environmentalists, business people and others went to Albany to lobby for the land bank. Considering that Montauk still had much land slated for development, CCOM urged its membership to vote in favor of it, and they did. Said Bill Akin, "Buying up land decreases density. And decreased density ensures better protection for the environment—more land for wildlife, more open vistas, more farmland, and better protection of our drinking water."

Assemblyman Fred Thiele marched the bill through the State Assembly and Senate. The Proposition was then vetoed by Governor Pataki in 1997 but he signed it in 1998 under great pressure from the East End. CCOM took the lead in the campaign in Montauk, while the GSF orchestrated the overall effort. From 2000 to 2005 East Hampton Town has directed $21 million of C.P.F. money to Montauk. It has been an important source of funding for open space preservation in Montauk, with several purchases on the CCOM "wish list" being realized and many others under consideration.

Fred Thiele, Kevin McDonald (of the Group for the South Fork), and Stewart Lowry (of the Nature Conservancy) were the driving forces behind the transfer tax—with a lot of help from the CCOM Board of Directors.

Ultimately the voters on the East End extended the tax from 10 to 20 years under the assumption that by then there would be very little left to save.

FOR THE PURE PLEASURE OF PRESERVING MONTAUK'S DRINKING WATER: A PARTY.

HITHER-WOODS 1777 ACRES SPECIAL RESERVE

DANCING TO THE JIM CHAPIN BAND. OPEN BAR AND BUFFET. THIRD HOUSE, EAST OF MONTAUK VILLAGE. RAIN OR SHINE. $20 PER PERSON—TAX DEDUCTIBLE DONATION.

5-7:30 P.M. SAT. JULY 4. DEEP HOLLOW RANCH.

CONCERNED CITIZENS OF MONTAUK

Chapter 4

Clean Water:
Lake Montauk,
Groundwater, and
Protecting the Coast

WHILE THE PRESERVATION OF MONTAUK'S OPEN SPACE has long been a priority for CCOM and its allies, of equal importance has been the protection of Montauk's underground water supply, freshwater lakes, and surrounding saltwater harbors, sound, and ocean. With the Atlantic Ocean to the south and Block Island Sound to the east and north, Montauk is surrounded by saltwater. Beneath the land surface is Montauk's natural freshwater aquifer, which is precariously thin and itself floating on salt water. And everywhere the peninsula is dotted with small ponds, sink holes, and freshwater lakes. Although receiving less public attention than Montauk's beaches and saltwater fishing, the aquifer, lakes, and wetlands are perhaps even more important to sustaining the ecological well-being of the area.

Unfortunately this fact was not recognized until after development started to surge in the late 1960s. Countless examples of poor planning—or just honest ignorance—made the job of protecting Montauk's freshwater aquifer and saltwater estuaries no easy task.

No body of water exemplifies this dilemma as well as Lake Montauk. Home to Montauk's ever-growing fleet of commercial and recreational fishing boats at its north end, and surrounded by private homes to the south, the Lake, as it is commonly known, is not a natural harbor. It was a freshwater lake, the largest on Long Island, until developer Carl Fisher dynamited a hole through the dunes in the 1920s to create a yacht harbor. As might have been expected, the limited tidal flow in the lake is not sufficient to handle the daily burden it is now exposed to. With fragile scallop and clam beds, a critical flounder spawning ground, and transition estuary for millions of tiny bait fish, Lake Montauk is challenged to accommodate the commercial and private development that now surrounds it.

Fort Pond Bay

Fort Pond Bay is unique. This half-mile bay to the north of Montauk is the deepest near-shore body of water on Long Island. For this reason it has been the site of a number of marine activities. Montauk's first fishing harbor was here, dating from the early twentieth century. Even as early as 1890, Long Island Railroad President Austin Corbin proposed Fort Pond Bay as the landing site for steamships. Just after World War II, it was suggested that it might be used as a submarine base and for offshore oil drilling. Most recently, Cross Sound Ferry has shown an interest in the Duryea Lobster House on the bay as a possible terminal for high-speed passenger ferry service from New London, Connecticut. But in 1973, it looked as if Fort Pond Bay might become home to a giant marina complex, including a 150-foot dock, despite the bay's wide-open exposure to storms and strong northerly winds. CCOM, along with the New York Ocean Science Laboratory situated on Fort Pond Bay, lodged objections to the Department of Environmental Conservation, and eventually brought suit against it.

Bill Dudine, a Manhattan patent attorney and CCOM board member, was the lead lawyer. "Bill was a brilliant guy who taught himself environmental law," says Russell Stein. Stein recalls that

> The DEC objected to our [CCOM] standing. There was a deal [made by Dudine] with the DEC, that in exchange for not challenging our standing, we would allow the case to be moved to Albany County

CCOM legal advisor Russell Stein.

where the judges were more friendly [to the DEC], removing it from Long Island. Bill had to fly up to Albany about 15 times.

What you have to know about the case is that this is the time when all of New York state's environmental laws were being written—the Wetlands Act, State Environmental Quality Review Act, etc. There was no SEQRA [then]. We were using older conservation laws, laws of administration, due process, openness procedures—anything we could get our hands on to prove that the DEC had approved this giant marina in Fort Pond Bay on the most pristine body of water left in New York State. Absolutely pristine; there were no pollutants at all!... [there was] no environmental impact study; that came later. We were grasping at straws... to show they [DEC] were arbitrary and capricious. They [DEC] exceeded their authority; made a decision based contrary to substantial evidence. It worked.

The Albany judge made a favorable decision... saying the DEC was totally out of line.

Carol Morrison states it simply. "They thought we didn't have a prayer because we had no standing in court," she says. "Well, we proved the reason for our standing was representing our community to protect the waters. We won."

When asked whether others were involved, Stein came up with an unusual post script: "[Perry] Duryea helped us [behind the scenes] because his business required clean water coming into his lobster tanks and going out again... We got the Ocean Science Lab to come up with data to say how wonderful the water was that they were bringing in, so that helped. I remember [Dudine] saying, 'But for the Ocean Science Lab, we would have lost.' We could say to the court that this [the Lab] was a state-funded asset that was about to be degraded."

The Suffolk County Water Authority and the Pipeline

Old-timers never said they were going *to* Montauk; they said they were going *on* Montauk. This is because they thought of Montauk not as an extension of East Hampton and Long Island, but because they viewed it as a separate island. Only a low, narrow five-mile stretch of sand dunes keeps the Atlantic Ocean from joining Block Island Sound along what is now commonly referred to as the Napeague stretch that connects Amagansett and Montauk. Hurricanes have periodically washed through at Napeague (most recently Hurricane Carol, in 1954), cutting Montauk off from the rest of Long Island. With innocence or ignorance, most people never thought that Napeague would be threatened by development, but the allure of pristine beaches and calm bay waters overcame any hesitation generated by common sense. Still, there was one problem not even stupidity could overcome: there was no fresh water supply.

CCOM's August 1979 newsletter warned:

> Motels will cover the open duneland to the south of the Montauk Highway. If the Napeague Motel District comes about as planned, we will have lost again. We will have lost to developers one of the most beautiful dune areas in the world.

Since no adequate source of potable water existed in the Napeague stretch, this gave the opponents of development a weapon to fight with.

The Napeague stretch had no natural source of fresh water. Motels and private homes were permitted and forced the extension of public water. The ocean cut through to the bay during hurricanes in 1938 and 1954.

A "Save Napeague" fundraising campaign, led by William King and the Amagansett Residents' Association, got underway. CCOM and others called for a Town water-management plan to be put into effect before any development on Napeague could take place.

In the spring of 1980, the Town enacted a six-month moratorium on hotel and motel construction on Napeague (and in Montauk at various sites: Fort Pond, Fort Pond Bay, and on the ocean at Ditch Plains). A total of 167 acres was affected. However, a 45-unit motel at Napeague was not affected, as it was in litigation. The Town voted to upzone 70 acres of oceanfront to one-acre residential and to condemn a 4.5-acre parcel in the middle of the tract under development.

But despite the success of the environmentalists at getting the Town to pay attention, there was a powerful stumbling block in the Suffolk County Water Authority (SCWA). At a CCOM meeting devoted to groundwater and the need for a groundwater management plan, audience members complained that long-term water supply plans were being made for Montauk without any local consultation, and that the SCWA should be made accountable to the Town Board. Audience members recall that a representative of the SCWA stood and said that the agency "was accountable only to God."

Authorities, created at the state level with "superpowers," can indeed override local laws. The SCWA is mandated to provide public water to those who ask for it, and it makes its money putting in mains and pipelines. The Suffolk County Health Department and the SCWA representatives stated unequivocally at public hearings that existing groundwater at Napeague would be sufficient for the planned development. Then, when that proved not to be the case, the SCWA laid a pipeline to supply the water, after having signed a contract to do so with the "Napeague Beach Improvement Corporation," an organization of private Napeague landowners.

As former Town Councilman Tom Ruhle put it, "The SCWA mission is simple: they like building water mains and the health department would approve almost anything.... They had literally stood up and said 'you can build the motels—no problem.' Next [thing] you know the motels are back, arguing 'We've got all these motels and the water is terrible.'"

The outcome of bringing public water to Napeague is apparent to anyone driving past Napeague's glut of motels and condos and blown-up, supersized homes.

Groundwater Management

CCOM saw that the pipeline could easily be brought to Montauk as well, and feared the potential for misuse and excessive overdevelopment. When there were reports of rusty water in the downtown area and of saltwater intrusion during summer droughts, some in the community called for public water.

Many on the board felt the organization should fight ferociously against it. Russell Stein noted that "They have helped make us a suburb. They had plans for 30 years to pipe all Long Island together, and now they've done it... It's a Faustian bargain. You get your water and you lose your soul [to suburbanization]."

But others, including Richard Kahn, disagreed that CCOM could successfully fight development using the water issue. He believed that zoning was the proper tool, not opposition to the SCWA.

After that contentious CCOM meeting devoted to groundwater—where the SCWA representative irked audience members with the statement about the SCWA's accountability—CCOM sent a letter to the Town Board:

> The Board of Directors of CCOM has spent many hours in recent months discussing, evaluating and questioning the explosive proliferation of development proposed for Montauk. We are particularly aware of the Sanctuary, Shadmoor, Lakeview Estates, the Surf Club condominium, the white elephant condominiums, and the Montauk Manor. We note major motel expansion in town and along Old Montauk Highway... CCOM asks the East Hampton Town Board to make any further final approval of major developments contingent upon immediately available and carefully allocated proven water supplies.

In a letter dated October 18, 1982 to Robert Lett, chairman of the Town Planning Board, CCOM President Richard Johnson wrote, "Concerned Citizens of Montauk concurs completely with the need to assess the potential supply of water for our community. It is essential for establishing parameters for development and its requirement for water." He pointed out that a water study by Rochris Associates was flawed because of the assumption that all soils are similar, which in Montauk is not the case. "As we all know, our only source of water is from the skies. This water needs to be stored." He closes with this admonition: "Knowing the topography is an essential ingredient in measuring the potential quantity of drinking water for an area."

The *East Hampton Star* reported in November 1982 on the persistence of contamination in groundwater by the pesticide Temik on both the South and North Forks of Long Island. Joseph Baier, chief of the County Bureau of Water Resources, explained that Temik pollution occurred primarily in the agricultural areas on the southern portion of the outwash plain of the East End, and that the contaminated water moved south. The implications concerning piped water from East

Hampton to Montauk became even more important with these revelations; unlike the farmed soil of East Hampton, Montauk was never an agricultural area.

A 12-point water resources management plan was written by Larry Penny and planner Lisa Liquori in 1987. "It said we shouldn't be extending public water where we don't need it," Penny recalls. "Private well water was of higher quality than the SCWA water in some areas. We felt that Montauk should be self-sufficient. Obviously it turned out that it wasn't self-sufficient." There had been big droughts, Penny explained, and when that happened "we started drawing salt water in Montauk."

The issue of groundwater continued to play an important role. The SCWA pipeline and the frequent seasonal crisis of Montauk's water supply fueled pressure to extend the pipeline to Montauk. CCOM's September 1997 annual meeting was devoted to the subject of water, with SCWA chairman Michael LoGrande attempting to allay concerns about the pipeline. CCOM maintained that conservation measures, land acquisition to protect water purity and reduce further demand, and the Hither Woods wells would be the appropriate solution to water demand.

But the battle to prevent the pipeline extension was lost. So CCOM tried to work with the SCWA to limit the amount that would be pumped into Montauk during the summer when demand was highest. The SCWA agreed to pump no more than 20 million gallons "except as needed for health, safety, or welfare concerns." This was a large loophole. Said Carol Morrison, chair of CCOM's liaison committee to the SCWA, "I keep track of it. We haven't finished the year [2004] and we're up to 35 million gallons." By 2005 the SCWA was calling for a meeting, saying they needed to pump significantly more.

In 1998, after much discussion, the SCWA won permission to extend a pipeline from Napeague and along the Old Montauk Highway with the following conditions:

1. The water be used [primarily] for emergency use

2. That controls be placed to limit the flow to 20 mil. gallons per year

3. That water not be transported west

4. That existing wells be maintained

5. That a water model be incorporated into the final EIS

6. That the SCWA issue no more certificates of availability

7. That the SCWA make money available to buy up land around well sites

8. That a master plan for Hither Woods be developed that included knowledge of how much water is available in the area

CCOM President Bill Akin sums up the current situation in a recent newsletter:

> Until 1998, 100% of Montauk's drinking water had been supplied from Montauk, i.e., our own aquifer. As demand increased, salt water began to seep into some SCWA wells (the source of Town water) and some private wells. To ensure a continued supply of fresh water and to provide water for emergency fire protection, Montauk was connected to the East Hampton aquifer via a water main. As a result of this connection, our local water supply is now supplemented to an ever-increasing extent from East Hampton. Unlike Montauk, East Hampton's aquifer is ample.
>
> So in Montauk the problem is quantity, but in East Hampton it is quality, and Montauk is now connected to East Hampton.

"There's almost nothing we can do to slow that flow of water down," Akin says today, when speaking of the pipeline through Napeague from East Hampton. "What we can do is point out the vulnerability Montauk has. God forbid if a big storm comes through and wipes that pipeline out—we're no longer supporting ourselves here."

There was another instance where insufficient groundwater and seemingly well-intentioned attempts resulted in unintended consequences. Supported by Harry Ellis and people on East Lake Drive, Steve Younger of the SCWA proposed running a pipeline under the Montauk harbor inlet. This required getting an easement from the Town of East Hampton, which owned the property on either side of the inlet where the new pipeline would connect. CCOM was concerned from the start that the new source of water might lead to the installation of showers, toilets, and more at the still-rural County Park.

With the Culloden Point Preserve and to the west (right) and the County and State Parks to the east (left) dense development surrounds Lake Montauk, a fragile fresh water lake opened up to Block Island Sound in 1927 by developer Carl Fisher.

Because of the SCWA's state-level authority, the Town would have no jurisdiction to control what additional hookups might result. CCOM met with Town Attorney Eric Bregman to insist that some mechanism be installed to prevent the SCWA from hooking up the County Park without any Town approval. Initially Bregman's opinion was that the Town had no jurisdiction, but Kahn convinced him otherwise. He reasoned that because an easement from the Town was necessary to get the pipeline over to East Lake Drive in the first place, the Town had the right to condition its grant of the easement on the Town's approval of future hookups. Perhaps more important, this provision would allow other entities to insist that the Town produce an Environmental Impact Statement before approving any environmentally controversial expansion plans. As it worked out, both the Town and the SCWA were quite open to this suggestion and this right was acknowledged in the final agreement to bring the water to East Lake.

In a karmic turn of events, shortly after the pipeline was installed, Inlet Seafood on East Lake Drive, long-time home to a portion of Montauk's commercial fishing fleet, proposed developing what looked at first like a slightly smaller copy of the Gosman restaurant and shopping complex located at the end of West Lake Drive on the opposite of the inlet. Harry Ellis, who had led the fight to bring water to East Lake, suddenly realized the downside to unlimited water and formed a new organization, the East Lake Drive Association. Worried about dramatic changes to their neighborhood and increased traffic, this new citizens' group set about meeting with lawyers in an effort to challenge the new complex. As of 2005 modifications have been made to the original Inlet Seafood proposal, but attempts to halt the project have been unsuccessful.

Lake Montauk

ARE THREE MILE HARBOR

AND LAKE MONTAUK

TO BECOME OPEN SEWERS?

This was the full-page ad published in the April 27, 1972 edition of the *East Hampton Star.* The ad called for a moratorium on zoning approvals affecting marinas in Montauk until "present pollution is eliminated." CCOM was part of a larger citizens' group that ran the ad. The ecosystem of the lake had become a concern as far back as 1964, when the Montauk Lake Club and Marina was purchased and docks, restaurants, a motel, and marinas were built in an area zoned for residential use, with owners attempting to circumvent zoning laws.

In December of 1981, Richard Johnson urged CCOM to consider the development of a policy for the lake. Soon thereafter a letter signed by CCOM President Dorothy Disken was sent to the Town Board and published in the *Star*:

> This year and in years to come it will be a first order of business for CCOM to investigate and document changing conditions on Lake Montauk, to promote and preserve the health of the lake and its environs and to give no quarter in the fight to prevent short term

exploitation to the detriment of future generations of Montaukers.... As soon as practicable [the Town] should establish a moratorium on all new uses likely to impact the lake for the duration of the study.

CCOM voted $1,000 toward starting up this project and pledged to use its resources to accomplish those objectives. Town Supervisor Mary Fallon acknowledged the communication but ignored the offer of $1,000 toward the project. A year later, following a report by Arthur Kunz of the county planning department in response to a request by the Town Board for a study on the lake, Fallon said, "We in no way want to jeopardize the ecological balance of the lake. The northern end has pollution and we want to resolve that. We want to monitor development closely." The county report concluded that development around the lake should be restricted, runoff controlled, and commercial fishing facilities limited to the north end where the lake opens into Block Island Sound. Little if anything was done by Fallon to reconcile her statement with action.

When Larry Penny became director of the Town's natural resources department in 1982, Lake Montauk was closed to shellfishing in several places, including the southern part. "What I started doing was coliform analysis on weekends.... Every weekend we'd have the bay constables, Jeff Havelick and Rich Lemay, collecting samples. We started to find out some interesting things. We tested after rainfalls. We found out that there were very high coliform levels mostly around the marinas in Lake Montauk." He goes on to say that after publicizing the finding, marina owners, Suffolk County Health Services, and the DEC weren't too happy with the report, as they should have been taking responsibility for the condition of the lake. (Penny attributes pump-out stations, tighter security at marinas, boater education, and the establishment of no-discharge zone—later successes—as the eventual outcomes of this early work.)

"People needed to be educated," said Tom Ruhle—who, besides being a former Town councilman and Planning Board member, had also been a commercial clammer growing up near the lake. He complained that people were using Lake Montauk as a giant sump; that water would hit the roads, go into the drainage system, and into the lake. "The lake isn't a big garbage can. I used to think these brochures and signs were useless, but they help. People used to catch these huge swordfish, take a picture and toss the heads and skeletons back into the lake. They don't do that now. The water quality has definitely improved; the clams have returned."

While most of the attention focused on the lake throughout the 1980s was limited to professionals, government officials, and some baymen, a few residents with homes fronting the lake had also been noticing the changes and were alarmed. One of these, Richard Kahn, eventually found his way onto the CCOM Board of Directors, where he has played a critical role in most of CCOM's post-1990 issues. His story starts with a walk one day in the County Park (before it became the County Park), where he happened to meet Hilda Lindley, who invited him in for a cup of tea. "She worked me over," he recalls, "saying, 'You mean you're a lawyer and you're not engaged in saving Montauk?'" Later, the noise and environmental damage from speeding jet skiers on the lake became an annoyance to Kahn, and he and his wife, Elaine, went door to door seeking signatures on a petition from homeowners around the lake. In one of these homes, CCOM was holding its monthly Board meeting. Kahn credits Tom Ruhle, during his tenure as Town councilman, with creating a 5 MPH speed limit in Lake Montauk. The speed limit did not last very long because of opposition from water skiers, but ultimately the jet skis were banned from the lake. "My involvement with CCOM was [initially] merely self-interest," Kahn says. He became a member of the board in the early 1990s.

In 1991 Rav Freidel suggested the CCOM board produce a video film on Lake Montauk. His motivation was to win the fishermen over to the idea of protecting the fish habitat. Along with Richard Kahn and Bill Akin, Freidel was attempting to build alliances with the fishermen and met frequently with the Harbor Association, headed by Joe Gaviola, and Arnold Leo, secretary of the Baymen's Association. "The thing nearest and dearest to everyone was this body of water... Lake Montauk is 1,000 acres... [at one time it] was teeming with life, with bay scallops; people couldn't believe what they tasted like! And of course, the eel grass, their habitat... needed to be protected." There is little

Protecting Lake Montauk has been a major part of CCOM's work. The north end of the Lake (foreground in both photos) is home to New York's busiest commercial fishing port while the majority of the Lake is surrounded by private homes and is a prime shellfish area.

doubt that the lake had been made vulnerable by Carl Fisher's vision of creating another Miami out of Montauk, which had entailed not only the opening of the north side but also the construction and recent expansion of the Yacht Club on Star Island.

Plans to kick off a "Save The Lake" campaign were initiated at CCOM's annual meeting in 1991. In conjunction with the campaign, Larry Penny sought financial support for a study of the lake to compare shellfish data with his early studies. *The Last Lake on Long Island*—the video suggested by Freidel—had its premiere at the meeting and successfully demonstrated the strains and stresses Lake Montauk was undergoing.

Included in the video was a demonstration of Richard Kahn's innovative, simple test of the lake's health. It involved checking his sea wall fronting the lake where the gulls dropped clams and scallops to facilitate their opening. "We used to be ankle-deep in shells," Kahn remembers, "but there has been a sharp decline over the past 15 years. Some scallops are still there, clams are the toughest so they're still there, but mussels have pretty much disappeared." Also in the video were Frances Lester from Amagansett, a bayman, and Montauk sports fisherman and renowned jazz musician Percy Heath. Rav Freidel recalls that the video, which was run several times on Long Island public television, was even seen in the Caribbean. "People called [Percy] from the Caribbean saying they didn't know he was an environmentalist! When the red-winged blackbirds returned to Montauk in the early spring, Percy would fish for flounder in the lake. His knowledge of the fishery was a help in that project."

"We spent three-fourths of a year filming," continues Freidel, "with the notion being, let's present this to the Town and get the Town serious about pollution from boats, from run-off, from the houses, anything that could help to protect the lake. It doesn't make any sense that we're 125 miles out in the ocean here, away from the major metropolitan area, and East Hampton has 25% of its waters closed to shell fishing... It doesn't make any sense that Lake Montauk should be strewn with gasoline; that there should be containers of teak cleaner and Clorox bottles floating in the little reeds along the shoreline. [They are] things that take life away."

The film project was deemed well worth the effort, given the awareness it raised. Town Supervisor Tony Bullock gave it a lot of publicity and sang its praises. Larry Penny remembers a recreational clammer who'd seen the film telling him that he wouldn't eat clams from the lake. "That was the first time I saw the tough guys around Montauk actually say, 'Yeah, you're right, we got to do something about Lake Montauk.' It had people saying things they usually wouldn't say."

Along with the Baymen's Association and the Group for the South Fork, CCOM drew up a 12-point preservation program for Lake Montauk in 1991.

1. Creation of a "no-discharge" zone with provisions for vigilant enforcement.

2. Retrofit of Town scavenger plant for acceptance of pumped-out wastes from boats and mandatory installation of pump-out facilities at all marinas.

3. Prohibition of all new construction in, or disturbance of, areas of eel grass meadows; study and implement methods of restoring eel grass beds and wetlands.

4. Expansion of existing marinas in north end of Lake Montauk to be conditioned upon substantial reduction in existing coliform counts.

5. Extension of 5-MPH harbor speed limit to the entire lake.

6. Overnight anchorage of transient boats to be limited to marinas only.

7. Assessment and elimination of leakage into lake from septic systems, possibly funded through partial tax credits, and control other sources of pollution within lake's watershed with specific emphasis on drainage through Peter's Run and from Oceanside, Steppingstone Pond to the Star Ranch area.

8. Elimination of road run-off from Town launching ramps and other points of entry into lake.

9. Restrictions of the use by lakeside and watershed residents of pesticides and other chemicals, including impregnated wood, that could adversely affect the viability of shellfish, finfish and wildlife populations.

10. Acquisition for nature preserves of the most environmentally sensitive and undeveloped lakeside parcels, including underwater parcels.

11. Recognize the lake south of Star Island as a priority shellfish and flounder harvesting and growing area. Continue restocking of shellfish populations and monitor water quality and assess stock and habitat on a regular schedule.

12. Develop educational programs, both for the schools and the general public, as to the importance of Lake Montauk and the steps necessary for its preservation.

"We wanted a Lake Montauk Harbor Management Plan to protect the South End of the lake," says Rav Freidel. "The lake is 1,000 acres. It is designated a New York State significant wildlife habitat. The plan would protect the north area of the lake as well. How many boats would be in the mooring area, where fueling and pump-out stations would be so that people wouldn't just jettison their head waste into the lake, which was one of the biggest problems. The Yacht Club, with its 50-foot yachts that were basically houseboats that never left the dock, was a major polluter on the south side of Star Island. We worked long and hard to try and get a no-discharge zone." He claims there was a great deal of support of people from diverse constituents, such as the Baymen, marina owners such as Henry Uhlein, Town offi-cials Tommy Knobel and Nancy McCaffery, Stuart Heath (a shell fish-erman who worked in Lake Montauk), the Harbor Association, John Beckworth, Harbormaster Bill Taylor, and the Montauk Boatmen's and Captain's Association.

Achieving the goal of a no-discharge zone would take some time, however. Other ecological concerns needed to be addressed as well. At a CCOM board meeting in 1995, Andrew Jones, a fisherman who was working with Carol Morrison on the Peconic Estuary Citizens Advisory Committee, discussed the winter flounder population of Lake Mon-tauk. He told the board that in the early 1980s a study had found the lake to be a prime nursery for these fish. Regulations limited fishing in order to increase spawning, but nothing had been done to improve the habitat. Jones was highly critical of the Peconic Estuary group, as it had never studied the effects of toxins in the water as part of the management plan for the Peconic Estuary. Even the smallest amount of poison could prevent fish from reproducing.

Rav Freidel recalls that he received a particularly harsh kind of education in connection with efforts to protect the lake and its fish:

> We got bayman Frances Lester to talk about his fike nets they put in Lake Montauk to catch flounder. Jeff Havelick, one of the bay constables, said, "You guys got to do something about the situation in the lake, because they're just taking flounder full of their eggs, and there are few flounder." Between what we learned from Francis Lester about how polluted the water was and how few fish he got, and what we got from Havelick who's saying the problem is with taking the fish that are spawning, I contacted Arnold Leo, head of the Baymen, and said, "Hey Arnold, how about you pull your nets out of the lake and give it a rest for a couple of years?" I spoke to the head of the DEC, Joe Zawicki, and he said the flounder are in severe decline throughout the northeast for lots of reasons.

Arnold apparently was surprised by the call. Freidel continues,

> Arnold calls me back and says, "The flounder stocks are fine, but we'll make a deal with you. We'll take our fikes [long hoop nets used for catching flounder] out of the lake if you can get the sport fishermen not to fish for flounder at the same time. We'll do this during the spawning season, which is in May." I said, oh, this is progress! I called Zawicki and said what do you think? He laughed and said, "the flounder don't spawn in May, they spawn in the coldest weather—December, January, February. That's when it will do some good."

Freidel comments wryly, "All of a sudden you learn that everybody's feathering their own nest. And nobody is looking out for the lake and its resources, although they swear they do."

CCOM's efforts to implement its 12-point plan for Lake Montauk continued throughout the 1990s, with some success. In June of 1999, for example, the lake was finally designated a no-discharge zone. Marine sewage could no longer be pumped overboard into the lake, and boaters were provided with pumpout facilities for holding tank waste. Enforcement was through voluntary boater participation and education, with harbormasters and bay constables monitoring compliance.

Lisa Grenci, who had become CCOM president the year before, was proud to have worked on that designation as part of a committee with councilwoman Nancy McCaffery, who was the Town Board liaison, and Ed Michels, the chief of Marine Patrol. "We met at the Coast Guard Station for maybe over a year. It took a two-year-plus lobbying effort to get the no-discharge zone. We set the course for a lot of communities on Long Island as well as in Connecticut when we passed the no-discharge zone in our harbors." Not being a fisherman, Grenci evidently found it to be a learning experience. "To sit down with the fishermen and everybody else for whom it was their livelihood opened my eyes to another faction of our society."

While Rav Freidel has been disappointed, feeling that not enough has been accomplished with that 1991 12-step plan, Richard Kahn believes that at least some of its goals were achieved. When asked what is primarily needed in the quest for a healthy lake, Kahn states tersely, "Enforcement is part of it." He notes that nothing has been done by the Town regarding toxic chemicals that pour into the lake from peoples' boats. Freidel concurs, and adds that there are few pump-out stations on the lake: "How much effluent is being pumped out of the boats and how responsible are the boatmen, I don't know. But when I go to Snug Harbor [Marina], I see boats from Connecticut soaping down, pouring Clorox all over the deck getting rid of fish stains. Clorox is poison. It's worse than what's coming out of the heads."

Kahn points to continuing problems with seepage from septic tanks, construction, and road run-off, "where the Town has been so inept with what has been done, though we spend a great deal of money. The Town [puts] the catch basins in the wrong place and then when they fill up they don't empty them." Part of the problem is a lack of coordination with other municipal departments; cleaning of the catch basins was left up to the highway superintendant, who has said that there's nothing in the budget to cover the cleanup.

Though CCOM has had some success with its lake management plan, overall Kahn views Lake Montauk as "one of our failures."

Past CCOM Presidents Rav Freidel (left) and Lisa Grenci (right).

Another failure he mentions is the marsh pond filtration system, which was the brainchild of Larry Penny. Rusty Leaver, who leases land from the county to run a ranch at Theodore Roosevelt Park, sponsored rock concerts in the early 1990s. Folksinger Paul Simon donated $25,000 of the proceeds from one of the concerts held in July, 1990, to be given to CCOM. CCOM decided it would use it as seed money for the marsh pond plan. The concept was to clean up the runoff between Ditch Plains and the lake through a system whereby marsh grasses would filter pollutants. Children were getting ear infections from coliform when they swam in the south end of the lake. As Rav Freidel explains it, "every time people flush their toilets in Ditch Plain it ends up in the south end of the lake. Larry decided we'd create all these ponds that will catch all the toilet flushings… and sunlight and salt would help kill the coliform and then it would naturally have cleaner water flow into the lake."

Ultimately the marsh pond management plan never took off—though the money is still earmarked for the project. What caused the failure of the plan? According to then-Supervisor Tony Bullock, "if Larry's plan goes through, Larry would be making water flow uphill... This marsh pond plan would flood basements over at Ditch Plains." Freidel provides an inside view of the trying demands of politics when working for change:

> Every time I talked about [the marsh plan] there were more studies, more meetings. [The] Administration changes, so you go through years worth of meetings with Tony Bullock and all of a sudden Tony Bullock is gone and Cathy Lester is involved, and you have your work with her and more meetings with the harbor masters and engineers, and everything becomes meetings and then they're out.... Who's got the energy to take them through it again and again?

CCOM also worked to replace the CCA (copper, chromium, arsenic) pilings with recycled plastic pilings as a test project. It was successful, but nobody from the Town government is even familiar with it today, and the idea of switching to plastic is dead in the water.

Both Freidel and Kahn view Larry Penny as a very creative environmentalist, but they have also been disappointed in his difficulty in following through on some of his inspired ideas. Freidel says that the marsh plan is essentially "stalemated because we can't go forward without DEC permits, which they apparently won't grant." That agency often puts up roadblocks, which would require more perseverance than Penny has so far demonstrated.

For his part, Penny believes that CCOM's efforts—if sometimes frustrating—have nevertheless had a positive effect on the health of the lake. He points to the return of the eelgrass as an example. (Eelgrass is essential to fish and shellfish habitat, particularly bay scallops, and so signals the health of a lake's ecosystem.) Unfortunately, in 2004 the Town Board, with Larry Penny's approval, opened Lake Montauk to scallop dredging, which destroys eelgrass beds. Penny did point out that clam rakes do just as much damage. Stuart Heath reported afterward that there weren't enough scallops to make a meal. Dan King,

President of the East Hampton Baymen's Association, moved his family to North Carolina in 2004, disgusted with the prospects of making a living on East End waters.

Richard Kahn adds that "whatever is affecting the lake, it seems to be getting worse." He suspects the problem is due to road run-off. Although eel grass seems to be growing on the east side, he reports that it is diminishing on the west side. "How much is due to nature and how much due to pollution is hard to tell." And then, too, there have been problems with the pump-out situation. Kahn says that the pump-out facility on Star Island was initially poorly sited. In the summer of 2002 there was no pump-out boat, because Carl Darenberg, who was running it as a private business, "disappeared" from the scene. Although it took longer than it should have, the Town assumed responsibility for operating the pump-out boat in 2005.

Recreation site, fishery, natural habitat—the many uses and users of Lake Montauk continue to debate its care. Freidel is one who views it as a shellfish and finfish nursery; describing a picture hanging on the wall at Inlet Seafood, of a giant bluefin tuna leaping out of the water to catch a big bluefish, he dubs it a graphic illustration of the food chain. Snappers (baby bluefish) come from Lake Montauk, and to Freidel this only underscores the need to protect it. And the eel grass—which some see as resurging, and others see as in decline—is the subaquatic vegetation and a vital link of the Montauk ecosystem. Its survival is central to another CCOM drama, the battle over Kalikow's dock.

Lake Montauk: The Kalikow Dock

The sandy point just south of the Montauk Yacht Club on Star Island was once pristine dunes and tern nursery. Today it is the site of a 16,000-square-foot mansion with two tennis courts and indoor and outdoor swimming pools owned by onetime New York City real estate developer, *New York Post* publisher, and current MTA Chairman Peter Kalikow. To complete the mansion, in 1988 Kalikow applied for permission to construct what Larry Penny characterized as "a huge dock to berth a huge boat." Kalikow "tried to get special approvals and started off with [asking for] a 420-foot "T"-shaped dock, plus finger piers, a swim float, and a boat house," Richard Kahn remembers. The dock would have accommodated Kalikow's 137-foot yacht and six other boats. His application precipitated a multi-year battle.

Although fixed docks had long been prohibited south of the Yacht Club on Star Island, floating docks were still allowed subject to obtaining a special permit. However, only three docks had been constructed in the south part of the lake, all before 1984 when the Town Code requirements were stiffened. CCOM was alarmed by Kalikow's proposal, not only because it would interfere with navigation and damage important eel grass beds but also because of the precedent it would set. Larry Penny calculated that, based on the number of waterfront parcels on the south end of the Lake, the potential proliferation of docks amounted to 157. John Aldred, director of the town's Shellfish Hatchery, noted the environmental damage that would ensue from spills of diesel fuel and antifreeze, bottom paints and boat cleaners.

Faced with strong opposition from CCOM and others, Kalikow scaled back his proposal and asked the ZBA to approve a shorter dock at an alternative location. Nevertheless the ZBA voted to deny the permit because of the adverse environmental impacts. However, before the decision was reduced to writing and filed with the Town Clerk, Kalikow's attorney contacted the Chairman of the ZBA with yet another modified proposal which, without the benefit of a public hearing, the ZBA accepted by a 3–2 vote. (Not so coincidentally CCOM member Lillian Disken, who served on the ZBA, was on vacation when the new proposal was discussed by the Board.)

CCOM engaged David Neufeld to challenge the ZBA decision in court. Joining in the suit were the East Hampton Baymen's Association, the Group for the South Fork and three individuals—CCOM directors Richard Kahn and Kay Carley and the President of the Baymen's Association, Dan King. Ten months later, in 1991, Justice Robert Doyle overturned the ZBA decision, principally on the ground that the fixed catwalk connecting the floating dock to the upland violated the Town Code's prohibition on fixed docks.

By this time, however, the dock (including the catwalk) had been completed. A stop-work order had been issued, but not before the work was finished. The only penalty that imposed was a $1,000 fine levied against one of Kalikow's corporations for failure to obtain a certificate of occupancy for the house. It now seemed to some CCOM members that Kalikow's strong political connections were coming into play. Richard Kahn reported that an aide to Congressman Michael Forbes had turned up at a meeting between NMFS and the Army Corps of Engineers to argue in favor of the dock, back when the two agencies were in discussions about required permits. The press reported that guests at the Kalikow mansion included U.S. Senator Alfonse D'Amato and his fiancée. In any event the Town Board, led by Supervisor Tony Bullock, enacted what CCOM promptly dubbed "The Peter Kalikow Relief Act of 1995." It legalized the illegal catwalk for what Rav Freidel called "an environmental criminal."

CCOM's newsletter of March 1995 sums up the situation:

> The application should never have been considered, since Mr. Kalikow has code violations pending. He has not had a certificate of occupancy for his residence since it was completed. Additionally, the ZBA allowed Mr. Kalikow to complete his estate in return for three easements meant to protect wetlands and ensure public access to Lake Montauk bottom lands. The easements have not been granted.

KALIKOW DOCK—WE TOLD YOU SO! the newsletter headline of January/February 1996 said. It summarized the report by the National Marine Fisheries Service (NMFS) stating that "habitat degradation resulting from the structure extends over approximately one acre... The overall impacts were larger and more pervasive than had been predicted during the evaluation process and the affected area is continuing to expand."

The follow-up was the July 1996 newsletter, which ran a black box with this headline:

INSULT TO INJURY DEPARTMENT
KALIKOW FINED $250.00

It noted that Judge Cahill granted Kalikow 12 postponements for illegally building the fixed catwalk without natural resources or building permits, and then fined him only that small amount. "This fine makes a sham of the fight to protect the lake from those who think they're above the law," the newsletter declared.

However, notwithstanding the existence of Kalikow's dock, the final outcome of this long struggle was a major victory for Lake Montauk. Perhaps out of embarrassment—Supervisor Bullock admitted he was "dismayed" and "annoyed" by Kalikow's "serious" violations—the Town Code provisions relating to floating docks were extensively revised and tightened under the leadership of Councilman (and bayman) Tom Knobel. In the 10 years following the legalization of Kalikow's dock, no new dock in the southern part of the lake has made it through the approval process.

With the Kalikow conflict CCOM again was reminded firsthand how frustrating it was to attempt to get the Town and other government agencies to enforce what appeared to be clear laws and to adhere to legal procedures. Probably no situation exemplifies this reality better than the extremely protracted dispute centered around a private home-turned-commercial-marina, known first as the Captain's Marina and later as the Lake Club.

Lake Montauk: The Captain's Marina

Built as a private house in the late 1920s, the Lake Club, also known as the Captain's Marina, on East Lake Drive (on the east side of Lake Montauk) has been the source of CCOM's longest continuous legal struggle. Even before CCOM was in existence, the house was sold to Robert Cohan, whose dream was to turn the location into a marina for expensive sportfishing boats and charter boats. Cohan began operating a commercial business in the early 1960s.

Opening the Captain's Marina created two problems. The first was a legal issue: certain commercial businesses, such as marinas, were permitted in "B Residential" zones (like East Lake Drive) only if they were located on a five-acre or larger parcel of land. The Captain's Marina was located on two upland acres with an additional three acres underwater. To many neighbors, and even the Town Zoning Board, this wet-and-dry interpretation of the law was not what was intended. Second, and certainly the more important issue, was that 40- and 50-foot high-powered sportfishing boats would have a major negative impact on Lake Montauk. Located a mile up the lake from the commercial harbor and inlet, the marina's boats would constantly be crossing over shallow eel grass beds, which were critical to the scallops and clams harvested from the lake.

As early as 1964, despite being denied a permit by the Zoning Board of appeals to use the premises for a multiple residence (such as a motel or inn), and one year after being denied permission to construct a swimming pool, bar, and public restaurant, Cohan utilized the "Montauk Option" (that is, "just do it") and built a pool. And the Town did what the Town usually did in those days—nothing.

By 1972, CCOM was up and running. The organization joined a suit brought by the Town to prohibit the marina from dredging to accommodate larger boats and to challenge the commercial operation of the restaurant, bar, and ship's store.

In 1973, State Supreme Court Justice De Luca agreed with the Town and CCOM and declared the operation to be illegal, but, in an attempt to "go easy" on the business, the judge urged the parties to reach a compromise. CCOM agreed to let the Captain's Marina phase out the operations over a two-year period if they would not appeal the court's decision. Captain's Marina agreed to the compromise but appealed the decision anyway. Justice De Luca next signed an order enjoining the operations, but the attorney representing the Town and CCOM, Howard Finkelstein, received almost no direction from the Town on how to proceed.

Nevertheless, the appellate division unanimously affirmed De Luca's ruling in May of 1974. CCOM brought pressure on councilwoman Mary Fallon, who introduced a resolution directing the Captain's Marina to comply and giving the Town Supervisor the power to engage an attorney to enforce the court's ruling.

But the headline in the July, 1974 CCOM newsletter told the whole story: BUSINESS IS GOING ON AS USUAL AT THE CAPTAIN'S MARINA. The article went on to explain how after seven years of illegal operation and four years of litigation, nothing had really changed.

Russell Stein comments that in that early period of CCOM's work,

"There were variances here [in Montauk] of enormous proportions. People on the Zoning Board of Appeals were trying to give away the store." When CCOM objected to the board's decision requiring Captain's Marina to give up the ship's store in five years instead of asking for immediate action, the owner converted the entire operation into a club. Looking back, Carol Morrison laments that "we made a big mistake when we fought the [Zoning Board] decision… What they did as a result is they made it a club because you could have a club in a residential area."

Having successfully dodged the zoning issue, the Captain's Marina operated under the radar until the 1990s when Omnibuild USA #1, Inc., whose frontman was Nicola Biase, bought the marina/club. It didn't take long before the new owners were proposing a massive dredging project to deepen the marina for bigger boats. By that time troubling signs were already showing up in Lake Montauk. Scallop harvests were declining, and the eel grass beds were rapidly receding. The last thing the fragile body of water needed was a fleet of 50-foot cruisers (standard size by then) cutting across from the harbor area.

Richard Kahn remembers that "they proposed to dredge 32,000 cubic yards of spoil and then dump it on the Benson Reservation in downtown Montauk"—the Benson Reservation which Biase had claimed was his to do with as he saw fit.[3] CCOM members turned out in force at the Zoning Board hearing to oppose the granting of the natural resources permit.

By the summer of 1999, the board had turned down the dredging and dock expansion for the second time. Supreme Court Justice Werner denied Biase's appeal. Also, the Lake Club's carriage house was limited to two units by the Zoning Board, and there was to be no expansion of the structure, so it could not be a motel. CCOM got all it wanted. The newsletter stated that the petition for the dredging "has just been dismissed and the ZBA's determination upheld." It was a victory for CCOM—and very good news for Lake Montauk. But once more the club was sold, in 2004, to the owners of the Royal Atlantic motel in down-

---

3. As noted in Chapter 3, in 1994 CCOM would support the several litigants in their fight against Biase's claim to the Benson Reservation.

town Montauk. Again "overflow" guests are finding themselves booked into the so-called "private" club.

Offshore Drilling

October 31, 1972
President Richard M. Nixon
The White House
Washington, D. C.

Dear President Nixon,

During the month of October you should have received over ten thousand letters requesting assurance that you will initiate measures to impede the issuance of offshore drilling leases on the Atlantic Continental Shelf. These letters were sent as a citizens' protest and were endorsed by fifty-six Long Island civic organizations who are now preparing newsletters to report your response to their members.

We ask now for your reply no later than Friday, November 4, as we must go to press on that date.

Helen Sarvis
Concerned Citizens of Montauk

CCOM vs. the United States Department of Interior can only be described as a contemporary tale of David and Goliath. The background of this amazing episode starts with the Army Corps of Engineers proposing in 1971 to locate a deep-water port off the shores of Long Island south of Montauk. They also proposed over 14 sites on Eastern Long Island for offshore discharge of oil boat carriers. CCOM board member Helen Sarvis had worked for an oil company early in her career, according to Dorothy Disken, and "she knew a lot more than the average person. She led that fight." Carol Morrison, who co-chaired the committee on oil, said that Sarvis was avid on the subject of offshore oil-drilling and that to her the thought of oil coming to Montauk via any method—boat, pipeline, tank farm, or refinery—was an outrage. Under her leadership, CCOM sent off over 14,000 letters to Washington.

CCOM had first held a meeting in 1971 to discuss the threat of oil drilling offshore. At a second meeting held in June of 1972, an obviously frustrated Sarvis declared,

> Since that time many of us have written to our congressmen and various lawmakers begging for a moratorium on drilling until an impartial study has been made of: ecological consequences, alternative energy sources and spill control technique. Various bills have been introduced into assemblies and Congress—there has been a hue and cry, but to our knowledge nothing concrete has been accomplished. We are still writing, we are still talking.

The reasons for the second meeting on oil were clearly delineated in CCOM's newsletter of June, 1972:

- Governor Rockefeller vetoed the State Shoreline Oil Spill Bill limiting drilling on offshore Long Island.
- The ACOE proposed a deep water port offshore Montauk Point.
- An *East Hampton Star* article [on March 1, 1973] stated that a 580-acre tract including 71 coastline acres currently zoned commercial had been sold to George G. Semerjian. [Semerjian was a Stony Brook industrialist who had a highly controversial joint mining-development project he had undertaken with the Curtiss–Wright Corporation at Jamesport and which he had later been forced by public and governmental pressure to abandon, according to reporter Jack Graves. The implications for oil storage facilities were strong.]
- Commercial zoning permits oil storage facilities.

There were many speakers at the June 1972 meeting, including Semerjian and Perry Duryea, then a member of the New York State Assembly. The bill had been drafted to help save Long Island waters in particular from major oil spills that had devastated large sections of California beaches. The *Daily News–Long Island* reported that "It was geared to protect the beaches from Coney Island to the Montauks." Rockefeller's veto "was filed at the closing hours of the last session of the Legislature, with the blessings of Republican Assembly Speaker Perry Duryea of Montauk." Executive Supervisor John V. Klein, also a speaker, was alone among the East End politicians to take a clear, unequivocal stand against oil drilling.

Kay Dayton relates that she "got in touch with a personal friend from the Department of Interior and he put me in touch with whom to talk to. There were a lot of us involved in that issue." Carol Morrison amplified:

> We ended up in court. The issue we were going for was an Environmental Impact Statement—we'd found out about Environmental Impact Statements. Bill Dudine defended our position against offshore oil drilling and the potential environmental damage of spills occurring during the transporting to land. He did a fantastic job in court, and it worked. The big thing we picked up on was: How are you going to bring the oil in from the rig out in the ocean to the land? Where was it going? There should be an EIS on that. It [the offshore drilling plan] never went anywhere.

OIL DRILLING TEST OFF L.I. DELAYED BY U.S. AGENCY was the headline of the *New York Times* on June 3, 1972. The story told how the United States Geological Survey had postponed exploratory test drilling into potential oil-bearing deposits on the Atlantic outer continental shelf for at least one year. It noted the "extensive opposition" by environmentalists all along the East Coast. "It is believed that this opposition, in past, was what led the [Nixon] Administration to postpone any further exploration or research pending a comprehensive study of the environmental impact statement."

"We are in the process of petitioning to the United States Supreme Court for a review of the environmental impact of ocean drilling and at the same time moving in the Court of Appeals for continuance of the injunction against further activity in the off-shore area pending completion of Supreme Court Review," declared the CCOM newsletter of September 1977. The Supreme Court refused to review the offshore oil case, despite the argument that it was one of the most important decisions affecting the area. In the newsletter of March 1978, it was stated that "now that we have exhausted our judicial remedies, we must focus on town, executive, and state governments to protect our environment." CCOM joined with Suffolk County Executive John Klein and the Suffolk County Legislature, Nassau County, and the Natural Resources Defense Council in a suit against the Department of Interior to block offshore drilling. The plan was eventually withdrawn, and the drilling was prohibited by Congress.

When asked what happened to change things, Russell Stein commented, "Other people got on board. That's what usually happens in politics. That's what I love about CCOM; it's usually the first. It's usually alone." Stein says that there was a political decision not to drill because Congressmen didn't want a challenge from the fishing industry, which had also gotten on board in the fight. Nancy Goell, of the Group for the South Fork, was appointed to the National Marine Fisheries Service when it was first formed in the mid-1970s. "For the first time there was an organized group of fishermen, and they would have none of it. They were absolutely opposed to the drilling," Stein says.

Also a concern in 1978 was whether Fort Pond Bay would be considered as an oil base. At issue was a finding by a bi-county coastal management study, which discovered that Fort Pond Bay was capable of handling a wide range of offshore oil facilities, with the industrially zoned strip on the southern part and a 50-acre sand pit parcel in the northwest corner. Lee Koppelman, executive director of the regional Planning Board, outraged CCOM. In considering the use of the bay as a potential site, he denied there was any departure from federal policy of total opposition to offshore oil drilling, saying that federal law required harbors with certain depths to be identified. An article in *Suffolk Life* reported that "the mere suggestion of a potential site for supporting offshore drilling was enough for the CCOM to formulate a strong reaction." Richard Johnson is quoted reading a press release following an emergency meeting of the organization. "We believe this recommendation is a betrayal of the public trust," he said. He promised that CCOM would garner all its resources to prevent offshore drilling from happening and that the organization would consider legal action. Though apparently there was no further action at the government level, this event certainly struck a note of warning to CCOM regarding bureaucratic behavior and the need for vigilance.

A JOB WELL DONE, proclaimed an editorial in the *East Hampton Star* in April of 1978.

> When Exxon's Glomar Pacific began operations, the case that Suffolk County and the CCOM had carried clear to the Supreme Court might have been considered closed... It was far from wasted effort.
>
> Very few people off Long Island had heard of CCOM until the fight against offshore oil began. This civic group, small by most standards although impressively large for the community it immediately serves, did a large job in its cooperation with Suffolk in legal action against the drilling.

The editorial went on to say that the struggle itself would deter oil companies from considering Montauk as an operational base. It also pointed to the major contribution of the suit in bringing attention to the consequences of offshore drilling and the ultimate responsibility for spills. The *Star* continued,

> It would have been unfair to expect the Concerned Citizens of Montauk, a small group with limited resources and what one might have expected to be a limited outlook, to have tackled this job and hung on to the bitter end as it did. But the Citizens persisted, and in doing so accomplished a good deal.

The article underscores an important dimension of CCOM: its persistence. And those with more than a nodding acquaintance with the organization would know that although CCOM was formed locally and acted most often to protect Montauk, the group's outlook is anything but limited. As the offshore drilling episode demonstrates, CCOM has implicitly defined itself as part of a larger environmental/ecological system. Obviously, what happens to the Manhattan or Connecticut waters and air affects Montauk, too.

Ocean Dumping

When you look at the CCOM logo you'll see a fish as one of four icons (the others are a bird, a plant, and water drop). Montauk is a fishing community with the largest fleet in many states. But the fisheries are in

Former CCOM President Rav Freidel.

severe decline both here and around the globe. There used to be sword-fish within a mile of Montauk. Today they're not within 100 miles. There are three major reasons for the demise of the fish: overfishing, indiscriminate killing of by-catch, and habitat destruction. So it was a natural segue for the organization to go from the microscopic to the macroscopic in its concern about water contamination, as everything is a part of the ecosystem. The dumping of toxic waste in the ocean and Long Island Sound became a new source of concern. In 1994, CCOM started an initiative against ocean dumping in the mouth of the Hudson River and Long Island Sound, which are some of the most important estuaries on the east coast.

The initiative was begun at the behest of Julie Evans-Brumm, an activist and part of the fishing community, who addressed CCOM's

April 1994 meeting and later joined the board. She described the government plans to deepen harbors around New York City and New Jersey, called the New York Bight, to increase trade by enabling new, larger container ships. But much of the sediment being dredged to deepen the harbors contained dioxin and other toxins. The government had been disposing of toxic sediment in the ocean, although such dumping had become illegal since the passage of the Marine Protection Resource Sanctuaries Act (MPRSA), called the Ocean Dumping Act in 1974. Nevertheless, there were still 40 outstanding permits to dump, which President Clinton was allowing to go forward. The EPA, which had the power to issue water-quality certificates and dumping permits, held the key to the process, she reported.

With considerable passion, Rav Freidel outlines this issue:

FISHERIES MEETING

In order to deal with the global subject of fisheries in crisis and to educate and create a local forum among those involved with fisheries, a general public meeting was held in September of 1994 under the chairmanship of Bill Akin. It was well publicized, very well attended, and involved local speakers: Dan King, a bayman; Michael Potts, a charter boat captain; Steve Sloan, a recreational fisherman; William Young, a surf caster; Ralph Owen, a commercial buyer representing longliners; and Chris Winkler, a Montauk dragger fisherman. In the September/October issue of the CCOM newsletter, an article asserted that "this was the first time an environmental group brought together the many factions of the Montauk fishing industry in an atmosphere of understanding and cooperation."

Prior to the meeting, Akin and his committee had distributed and collected questionnaires to 150 fishermen to investigate their views on key fishery issues as well as on how fishing had changed. Montauk is New York State's most important commercial fishing area, and recreational fishing is also key. Clearly the viability of the community was at stake. Most fishermen surveyed were pessimistic about the industry's future unless significant changes were

We started to get calls about the mud dump, and it is 100 miles from here. It is between Coney Island and Sandy Hook.... this is a toxic dump site for the Hudson River dredge spoils. The fish that pass through it are the same fish migrating north, following the bait fish, that we catch in Montauk. What happens when the bait fish get into this toxic pool? They get sick, they get weak, they get very vulnerable to the larger fish. All the species get sick from the bioaccumulating toxins—as do birds, turtles, dolphins, and, ultimately, people.

Freidel makes the point that what is objected to is not dredging, but dumping the toxic waste into the water. He complains that because the Jones Act—which disallows the operation of boats and technologies not made in America—"we're using antiquated equipment." The

implemented. Only 22% believed it would improve in the coming 10 years, and only 15% said they would encourage their children to make a living from fishing in Montauk.

Not all of the news was gloomy. Some hope was voiced at the meeting about the partial recovery of striped bass, thanks to drastic conservation methods that had been put into effect. Also noted was the available technology to farm bluefin tuna, fluke, and abalone to be released into the ocean—a potential if partial solution to over-fishing. Congressman Hochenbrueckner challenged the audience to give him a consensus representing the mutual ground of all represented, and promised to see the achievement of those goals. The newsletter summed up: "CCOM hopes that the survey and forum was a first step, and is committed to working with the fishing community to help find solutions."

An insert in the same newsletter urged members to write letters to Governor Cuomo about preventing the dumping of toxic dredge spoils into the New York BIGHT, the fertile mouth of the Hudson. The newsletter connected all the negative ecological dots: "Dumping [is] at the expense of the ocean, our health, and the livelihoods of East End fishermen."

result? "When these clamshell buckets from the 1890s go into a wetland area to dredge, the silt flows out and redisburses in the water
column and the lightest of all materials carry most of the toxins, so it's
all disbursed in the area you just dredged. And when the spoils are
dumped the same thing occurs."

It is now commonly understood that pollution as far away as the
Hudson River effectively destroyed the striped bass fishing in Montauk. As a consequence, CCOM expanded its horizons in terms of water
protection and took up this regional concern in order to work toward
maintaining Montauk as a fishing town. It became part of a coalition
whose reach extended from Montauk to Cape May.

Then a new variation on the dumping theme emerged, this time
much closer to home. Knowing that the ocean would soon become off-
limits, the government planned to deposit toxic spoil just north of
Montauk. In 1995, CCOM joined a suit brought by a coalition of groups
against the U.S. Navy, for dredging 1.5 million cubic yards of contaminated soil from Connecticut's Thames River and dumping it into Long
Island Sound in the Race, the deep-water channel where the Sound
and the Atlantic Ocean meet. There were more than 10,000 lobster pots
in the area, many from Montauk lobstermen. The suit was an injunction and claimed that the sediment had not been tested adequately, as
it was coming from five separate Superfund sites, but the Federal District Court judge ruled that the plaintiffs had not proven this. In fact,
the Navy, Army Corps of Engineers, Connecticut DEP, and the EPA tied
the hearing up long enough for the dredging project to be completed.
They even dredged and dumped nonstop through a raging December
nor'easter with 50-MPH winds.

Besides CCOM, the plaintiffs included Congressman Michael
Forbes, Fish Unlimited, the Long Island Sound Lobstermen's Association, and the North Shore Baymen's Association. In March of that year,
Rav Freidel attended a press conference held by Congressman Forbes
to announce proposed legislation to close a loophole in the ocean
dumping law by holding dumping into the Sound to the same stan-
dards as in the ocean—that is, effectively disallowing it. In the meantime, CCOM and others were outraged to learn that the Environmental
Protection Agency was rewriting its own regulations to make prior

CCOM protests NAYY dumping of dredge spoils in the Race. (Sept. 1997).

dumping activities legal. Also, the agency was trying to expand the mud dump site at the other end of Long Island from two square miles to twenty-three square miles and weaken the criteria for what is considered toxic. All this in spite of the fact that lobsters from the area had been shown to contain dioxin.

To drum up support in its fight to prevent the dumping, a committee chaired by Julie Evans-Braum and Rav Freidel was formed by CCOM in 1997. They successfully organized a broad-based flotilla to protest the dumping by the U.S. Navy of contaminated dredge spoils from the Sea Wolf submarine project into the Sound. Joining these efforts were the Montauk Boatman's and Captains Association, the Montauk Chamber of Commerce, the Montauk Harbor Association, the East Hampton Town Board, the North Shore Baymen's Association, the Long Island Sound Lobsterman's Association, and the Town of Southold. The boats headed out to a key fishing area in the Sound known as the Race, crammed with protestors holding large signs saying, "DON'T MUCK UP OUR FISH!"

"It's a very frustrating thing; it's still going on," says Bill Akin. "It's absurd to think you're not allowed to dump 80 miles off shore, but you are allowed to dump in Long Island Sound." He points to the 200 years'

CCOM members aboard the Viking Starship head a flotilla to protest dumping in Long Island Sound.

worth of industrial waste deposited in Connecticut rivers that are being dredged and says with incredulity, "to think you can dump this in the Sound where we already have the lobsters in decline radically, their shells in horrible condition, and the fisheries have declined."

The ocean dumping issue continued into the new century with the formation of a new group, the Friends of Long Island Sound (FLIS), in 2000 by Rav Freidel and Julie Evans-Brumm. Member organizations of the group include the Coast Alliance, the American Littoral Society, Clean Ocean Action, Fishers Island Conservancy, and the North Fork Environmental Council.

"We are afraid we will have more health advisories regarding fish consumption and more economic hardship for our fishermen if the dumping of toxins continues in Long Island Sound," wrote Evans-Brumm in a featured newsletter article in January, 2000 about the fledgling group. She wrote that the Army Corps of Engineers and the EPA were looking at dump sites besides Long Island Sound, including Block Island Sound, the Peconic Estuary, and the waters near Montauk.

Four years later, in early December of 2003, an action alert by the new group signaled a need for prompt action by concerned citizens, as the comment period on plans to dump 20 million cubic yards of toxic dredged material from Connecticut was coming to a halt. Thanks to the work of FLIS and other groups in exerting political pressure, Suffolk County's Steve Levy took up the banner for clean water and Senator Charles Schumer became actively involved as well, challenging a study which he says "underestimates the damage to the Sound." A *New York Times* article on May 26, 2004 about the Long Island Sound dumping plan reported that "Mr. Schumer and officials from Nassau and Suffolk Counties have said they will sue to stop the dumping."

At a CCOM board meeting in June 2004, Julie Evans-Brumm declared that "CCOM has another victory to add to the list!" Just the day before she had attended a press conference given by Randy Daniels, the New York Secretary of State. He announced that the Department of State had determined that the proposal by the EPA and the Army Corps of Engineers to allow dredged material dump sites in the Long Island Sound was inconsistent with the state's coastal policies. He indicated that New York did not support and would not approve the proposal.

In announcing this positive development, a FLIS press release credited Governor George Pataki, Suffolk County Legislator Steve Levy, Congressman Tim Bishop, and former Congressman Mike Forbes, and especially "the many individuals and organizations who fought this battle for the past 20 years," citing CCOM's participation as "their finest moment."

CCOM felt that concentrating on habitat destruction would give them standing with the fishermen in the community. Unfortunately, overfishing, by-catch destruction, and pollution continue to empty the oceans of fish globally as well as locally. What will happen to Montauk? Perry Duryea said, in promoting new uses for Camp Hero State Park, "build more golf courses, the fish are gone."

Chapter 5

The Town

and Beyond:

Other Concerns

A
S EVIDENCED BY CCOM'S INVOLVEMENT with the fight against off-shore drilling, the organization's concerns may have origi-nated in Montauk, but they extended far beyond the limits of that locale. And given the group's persistence in pursuing cases that took years—often decades—of organizing, fundraising, public aware-ness, and legal battles, they were well suited to issues with a larger environmental impact. From the 1970s and into the booming 1980s, through the 1990s and to the present day in the early years of the 21st century, CCOM continues its focus on preserving the land, water, and air of Montauk and beyond. Following are three issues emblematic of the group's broader concerns.

The Shoreham Nuclear Power Plant

What better way to demonstrate concern for the environment than to express a little civil disobedience? Several CCOM members recall well the organization's opposition to the opening of both the Jamesport and Shoreham nuclear power plants.

Russell Stein remembers that

> One of the earliest meetings I remember was at Hilda Lindley's
> house. We were up there on a beautiful spring day and Lorna
> Saltzman of the Friends of the Earth was there to talk to us for an
> hour about nuclear power. None of us knew anything about the
> downside. When she finished talking about Shoreham and also
> Jamesport [where LILCO wanted to put up two nuclear power
> plants], it became our Number One topic. CCOM took off on the
> nuclear plant issue from then on. That might have been our first
> out-of-town topic. I was surprised she was there to talk about it as
> it was an issue that didn't directly affect Montauk... I remember
> that sunny day and that doomsday scenario.

As Carol Morrison remembers it,

> My brother was pro-nuclear, so I thought nuclear [energy] was the
> greatest thing, as he kept saying, "Soon we won't be paying any-
> thing for electricity. It's just wonderful!" After hearing Lorna that
> Saturday morning, we all walked down the hill and I can still
> remember talking to Jim Proctor and... we all had our eyes opened.
> That was the beginning of being very, very active about Shore-
> ham... The concreteness of the impossibility of an evacuation plan
> was certainly a major factor. But also, the whistle-blowers came on
> the scene, talking about the shoddiness of the construction. It was
> a long time before we stopped it. People like [board member] Dick
> Johnson and Carol Anderson actually were put in jail because they
> tied themselves to the [Shoreham] fence. Oh, we were active!

CCOM member Carol Anderson's account of her experience of civil
disobedience and being arrested with her "band of nine, with an average age of 43," was published in CCOM's June 1979 newsletter.
Having been arrested after chaining themselves to the fence at Shoreham, she wrote,

> Exhausted and hungry, we shivered in our wet, filthy clothes.
> Handcuffed to each other, we sprawled on the floor of a large
> detention room. Stripped of our glasses and cigarettes, indeed of

Former President Richard Johnson.

all our belongings, we waited through the long night... What did we accomplish? Time will tell.

"We were street fighters then," Richard Johnson says almost wistfully. He had been very much in the leadership position on the issue, mobilizing CCOM pickets at Nuclear Regulatory Committee hearings and at the Shoreham No Nuke rally, connecting the group with the Eastern Suffolk Safe Energy coalition and challenging the Public Service Commission regarding the Long Island Lighting Company's (LILCO) promotion of nuclear energy plants at the expense of consumers. At the same time, CCOM was working to promote energy conservation locally by introducing the concept of solar energy and windmills at meetings.

Asked how CCOM participation was viewed in Montauk, Carol Morrison noted that,

Some people didn't like the idea... but we had a pretty good following. We became more popular at that time—that was the beginning, you might say of our popularity.... We needed [to do] fund
raising for our lawyer, Yaconne. There were strong feelings about
Shoreham because the first [nuclear plant opposition] we won was
Jamesport... There was going to be a nuclear plant there. We won
that one before they even started. Meanwhile, Shoreham was pro-
gressing to the point that it was [going to be turned] on.

According to Dorothy Disken, there was a lot of contention over the
Shoreham nuclear plant.

A lot of people owned stock in LILCO and they couldn't understand why—what harm was there? I remember someone saying to
me, "You don't really think you're going to stop that." I said I certainly hope to keep fighting and we did eventually win.

I remember they gave me a placard to hold and [there was] a picture of me on the front page of *Newsday*. I was hoping none of my
friends from the city would see me. Tom Twomey was marvelous
as we moved into court. He held up vegetables and said, "What are
we going to do with these when we have a [radiation] spill? Who's
going to buy vegetables from Long Island?"

Board member Maria Lubinska came to a protest meeting holding a
sign that said, FISH, NOT FISSION! remembers Russell Stein, who also
recalls learning about civil disobedience at training meetings run by
the Shad Alliance, an anti-Shoreham group.

I remember a wonderful debate between Charlie Raebeck and a
LILCO guy in the basement of Southampton Inn, [so packed] we
couldn't get another person in there. They were debating nuclear
power. (Charlie was the guy who I believe invented the slogan "No
Nukes.") After an hour of whipping the guy, some frustrated fellow
in the group from LILCO in the front row said, "We all got to go
sometime."... I'm sure that everybody in CCOM was urged to participate and did. What we had was an incredible board. They were
primed and ready to man the barricades, and did.

An important contribution to that awareness of the membership was as a result of the 1978 All-Suffolk Citizens' Environmental Conference organized by CCOM. It was a brilliant and most timely effort initiated by Hilda Lindley and Kay Dayton to explore and educate the public on the complex issue of sustainable energy. The welcoming speaker was Vice President William Dudine. Over 300 people attended, with 60 environmental groups represented. The topic was "The Environment and the Economy," which drew a significant group of public officials including New York DEC Commissioner Otis Pike, Peter A. Berle, Suffolk County Legislator Joyce Burland, and New York State Assemblyman Perry Duryea as well as an impressive panel of energy specialists. The keynote speaker was Harvard University Nobel Laureate Dr. George Wald.

Carol Morrison recalls the event with great satisfaction. "It lasted all day. Paula Procter was [in charge] of making box lunches. We all pulled together to make lunches for all those people. We were trying to make people aware of the dangers of nuclear [energy]." When asked why there was no follow-up conference, Carol Morrison replied, "Because there was no Hilda Lindley, with her amazing range of contacts."

"Time did tell," to paraphrase Shoreham activist Carol Anderson. The Shoreham plant was never opened, though the struggle continued. At CCOM's ninth annual meeting in July of 1979, County Supervisor John V. N. Klein suggested strongly that he would oppose the opening of the Shoreham plant under any conditions, although two years earlier he had been in support of the plant's opening. This change was a result of his visit to and study of the disaster in Three Mile Island, Pennsylvania. CCOM continued to educate and urge its members to actively work for the shutting down of the nuclear plant—and when Shoreham was closed, CCOM was proud to have participated in the effort.

The Ferry Threat

Montauk is at the east end of 120 miles of crowded highways and progressively more densely populated towns called Long Island. It also lies 18 miles south across Block Island Sound from New London, Connecticut. But to make the Montauk/New London trip, motorists have to either drive to Riverhead and then out to Orient Point—more than an hour's drive—or make the double local ferry connection from the Forks across Shelter Island, then on to Greenport, and finally out to Orient Point where the giant Cross Sound ferries depart. One long-standing exception has been the limited summer service offered by the small local passenger ferry operated by the Montauk-based Viking Fleet. Any large-scale direct service has been a serious but almost unanimously opposed idea in Montauk.

The issue gained steam in the 1980s—during the time of the East End's booming expansion. In 1984, there were several ferry operators eager to run ferries from Connecticut to Montauk. One service was proposed by the Groton–Montauk Ferry Service, which proposed a ferry dock at Fort Pond Bay next to the New York Ocean Science Laboratory. Another was proposed by Cross Sound Ferry Company, with mooring at Mid-Atlantic Seafood Buyers on East Lake Drive. CCOM was strongly opposed to both proposals. The newsletter of May 1984 questioned what traffic would be like in the inlet of Lake Montauk with "a large boat entering and departing three times a day." It also brought up parking and traffic issues on East Lake Drive, as well as shelter and sanitary facilities. All of this required Planning Board approval and an Environmental Impact Statement. The Citizens Advisory Committee voted against it, and the ferry proposal didn't happen.

In 1992, an attempt to develop a passenger car ferry on state parkland in Napeague, once home to the Smithmeal Fish Factory, was thwarted by the Town Board and opposed by CCOM and others. It was seen as adversely affecting the rural residential community by potentially increasing traffic and damaging fragile wetlands and marine life in Napeague Bay and Gardiner's Bay. Moreover, it was argued that the proposal contradicted the original purpose of purchasing parkland for habitat protection and enhancement. A plan for a car ferry into Lake Montauk had also been proposed, which was seen as equally disastrous. In November of 1992 the Town Attorney ruled that the Town Code banned car ferries in all enclosed harbors. As the CCOM newsletter reported, "the latest ferry proposal from New London to Montauk is for service four times daily. Each boat would discharge 24 cars.... Some Town officials believe that under Interstate Commerce

Commission rules, once a terminal is established, all local control over the ferry service is gone." As with the 1984 proposals, these did not pass either.

The ferry threat of the 1990s was of a different order of magnitude. There were two reasons for this. First, the Mashantucket Pequot Tribal Nation had opened the Foxwoods Casino near New London—it was the largest resort casino in the world and attracted more than 40,000 guests per day. If only a small fraction of those visitors decided to extend their gambling excursion to include a visit to Long Island's South Fork, the fragile environment of Montauk, its recreational facilities and parks, and its infrastructure, would be overwhelmed. Second, new technology had resulted in the development of high-speed, high-capacity ferries—Cross Sound Ferry was introducing a 400-passenger ferry with a cruising speed of 30 miles per hour, crossing from New London to Orient Point six times a day. The trip between Montauk and New London takes an hour and 45 minutes on the existing Viking Ferry; the new ferries could make that trip in less than half that time.

During the course of the ferry battle of the 1990s, the impact of high-speed ferries on the North Fork was a constant reminder of the damage they could do, especially because the New London ferry terminal was linked by privately chartered buses taking passengers directly to and from the Foxwoods Casino. The Town of Southold had been unsuccessful in obtaining a court injunction against the new service, and in the ensuing months the two-lane highway to and from the Orient Point terminal became clogged with traffic. Cars were parked along the local streets, residents were unable to exit their driveways, and "For Sale" signs sprouted up in front of houses along the route. The North Fork experience was especially pertinent because Cross Sound Ferry had demonstrated its disdain for the welfare of the community—if a service was profitable, Cross Sound would provide it irrespective of local impact.

But three years later, in the summer of 1995, the *East Hampton Star* reported on rumors about negotiations between the Duryea family and Cross Sound Ferry for a high-speed passenger ferry to New England from Fort Pond Bay. The newspaper noted the converging interests of the owners of Foxwoods casino in Connecticut and the

Cross Sound Ferry to bring people to the casino. Though East Hampton code essentially forbade car ferries in enclosed harbors, Montauk's Fort Pond Bay, with its deep water and the Duryea property on the bay, was zoned commercial waterfront. This increased the potential for a terminal construction.

With the publication of the *Star* article, light bulbs started flashing warning signs among a number of residents near the Duryea lobster business. In 1993 these homeowners woke to find Tuthill Road, their main access to town, blocked off (see Tuthill Pond sidebar). Apparently the Duryea family was exercising what they said was their right to close the road to validate their claim that it was their private road. Tuthill Road residents organized the Tuthill Road Association to fight the closure, but according to Lisa Grenci, one of the organization's leaders, East Hampton Town was very reluctant to take any action because the Duryea family was extremely well-connected politically. But when the news of the possible ferry terminal broke, the road closure issue suddenly seemed to be an integral part of a much bigger and more sinister scenario.

Grenci soon learned that the Duryea family had met with the Long Island Railroad and the New London-based Cross Sound Ferry Company with regard to establishing a ferry terminal at the site of the long-established lobster business. With little experience in dealing with issues having the potential impact of a Duryea/Fort Pond Bay ferry terminal, Grenci and the Tuthill Road Association appealed to CCOM for advice.

On one level, the Tuthill Road neighbors were rightly focused on the road closure as a cornerstone for the ferry operation. Grenci came to a CCOM board meeting and laid out her case. "Look, I've found all this information, and we need your help," she said. CCOM quickly explained how the Town Code dealt with ferry terminals and said that traffic management was as important as the road closure issue.

At a CCOM board meeting on July 1, 1995, Richard Kahn pointed out that stopping the ferry was linked to the overall dilemma of moving people on the South Fork. "It has to be the number-one priority," he said, "as this could destroy 25 years of environmental effort." The possibility of a major ferry service between New London and Montauk clearly involved significant legal issues and would impact all the communities on the South Fork.

Very early on, it was apparent that the funds necessary to defend against the ferry threat would far exceed CCOM's resources. A Stop the Ferry steering committee was formed that brought together people from all the East End communities. CCOM members Larry Smith, Bill Akin, Eugene White, Rav Freidel, Lisa Grenci, and Richard Kahn, among others, were joined on the steering committee by citizen leaders from Amagansett and East Hampton. This nucleus group in turn got the word out from Southampton to Montauk, and funds started rolling in. "One day we were a small group of Montaukers sitting around the firehouse," recalls Akin. "The next day we are sitting in a living room in an East Hampton beach mansion talking to 30 very wealthy and concerned people none of us had ever met before."

STOP THE FERRY bumper stickers started appearing on cars everywhere. Newspapers from New York to Montauk picked up on the issue. And finally, East Hampton politicians jumped on board, realizing how strong public opposition was to the potential of massive crowds of New Englanders suddenly invading local beaches and roads.

Much closer to home, the Tuthill Road Association (TRA) was still locked in a battle to ensure continued access on Tuthill Road. Furthermore, along with CCOM, the TRA was attempting to get the Town to take some action to slow the expansion of a restaurant and shops that started popping up at the old Duryea lobster business in apparent violation of the local zoning code.

The issue of whether the ferry would come to Montauk continued. It was not an easy task to deal with. Proponents of the ferry had engaged attorneys who argued that the Town could not prohibit the establishment of new ferry services because the Town could not regulate interstate commerce. Nevertheless, CCOM took the drastic step of calling for a moratorium on the approval of any new ferry terminals or the expansion of the existing terminal. "Towns hate to put in moratoriums because it just stops everything in its tracks," Richard Kahn says. "You have to have a very good reason." When the moratorium was called for in July of 1995, the Town Board, under Tony Bullock, unanimously rejected the idea. "I think it was a surprise that they had not really thought through what a fast ferry would mean," Kahn says. However, by October, when candidates were running for election, every one of them was outdoing the other in opposition to the ferry.

The moratorium was passed in November 1995. Concurrently with the moratorium, the Town authorized a 15-month traffic study to be undertaken by independent engineers. There was considerable anxiety expressed by the CCOM board that Mclean Associates, the consultants on the transportation study, might consider waterways as a solution to local traffic congestion. But they quickly recognized that a ferry would bring in extra traffic. The traffic study was comprehensive, covering levels of service on every road in Montauk and how they locked into

TUTHILL POND

Tuthill Pond is an environmentally fragile freshwater pond bordered by the Duryea lobster business, private homes, and pristine wetlands. At one point it is a mere 35 yards from Fort Pond Bay. The combination of a possible ferry terminal and the apparent unauthorized expansion of a restaurant and shops at what had been for decades the Duryea wholesale lobster distribution and ice house business threatened the purity of both Tuthill Pond and Fort Pond Bay.

In many ways the Tuthill Road closure and Lobster Deck expansion could be seen as tied to the ferry issue, but the more immediate environmental threat was the proximity to Tuthill Pond and Fort Pond Bay. As Lisa Grenci put it, "The restaurant was built over 50% tidal wetlands without either site plan approval or environmental review." Shops were later added, again without the proper review procedure being followed.

CCOM had to consider to what extent the Tuthill Road closure, the threat to the freshwater pond, and the fight against the ferry were linked. It became clear that the environmental concerns about the pond, Fort Pond Bay, and the Duryea expansion, potentially related to the ferry, were by themselves significant enough to justify a second front.

CCOM hired a hydrological engineer and the law firm of Twomey, Latham, Shea, and Kelley to investigate some of the issues. As intersections; it projected severe, adverse traffic impacts from new ferries. Kahn continued,

> Then the question: what kind of legislation? You don't want to unduly interfere with interstate commerce. We also didn't want to put out of business the existing ferry [Forsberg's company], which the community thinks is important. The only power the Town had was its zoning power—plus a little-known provision of state law that towns could regulate horsepower and boats within certain distances of the shore.

some years earlier the well closest to the restaurant had suffered from saltwater intrusion, one question was the source of the restaurant's water. CCOM's engineer and lawyer met with Interscience, Duryea's representative, who suggested they visit the site. The Interscience engineer pointed out two wells that he claimed were the source of the restaurant's water. Upon the CCOM engineer's insistence, the first well house was opened and the well was shown to be clearly abandoned. The Interscience engineer then asked Chip Duryea where the water came from. Duryea indicated the second well, but when examined, it was also clearly abandoned. CCOM's lawyer reported that the CCOM engineer said to the Interscience engineer, "Do you really want to know where the water comes from?" From there they marched up a hill, off the site, and onto a piece of property owned by the Duryeas but not contiguous to the restaurant property, from which a pipe emerged that went clear across Tuthill Pond on floats. He said, "This is where your water comes from."

It took until 2002 for the Tuthill Road Association to win their right of access over Tuthill Road. Shops are still operating without final approval, although the pipe has been removed from Tuthill Pond. It is reported that the East Hampton Planning Board has recommended that the one way to safely supply the restaurant with clean water is to extend a public water main from a half-mile away.

Richard Kahn, CCOM legal advisor.

The Stop the Ferry coalition engaged Michael Gerrard, of the Washington, D.C. and New York City law firm of Arnold & Porter, to work with Russell Stein to advise as to new zoning regulations which would both protect the town from the traffic impacts predicted by the study—and also be sustained by the courts as a reasonable exercise of the Town's legislative powers.

The legislation affecting high-speed passenger ferries, principally drafted by Rick Whalen, was enacted in 1997. It did not prohibit new ferry terminals, but did require the Planning Board to determine that there would be no severe adverse traffic impacts before it approved any such application. In the case of vehicle ferries, in 1995 the Town had enacted a ban on establishing terminals for such ferries in Fort Pond

Bay. Stop the Ferry found itself in the peculiar position of opposing the vehicle ferry legislation—because an outright prohibition is more difficult to sustain in court than are restrictions based on the impacts predicted in a traffic study.

"A fast ferry from Connecticut to Montauk would have been the end of Montauk as we know it," Richard Kahn says. A fast ferry would mean that New England would be only 50 minutes away. The number of day-trippers going to the beaches and the Hamptons would increase. Two high-speed ferries could discharge 4,800 passengers per day—more than the year-round population of Montauk. Landing at Fort Pond Bay, they would have to get to the ocean. This would mean bus transportation (or perhaps huge fleets of mopeds)—as well as t-shirt shops, fast-food shops, convenience stories, and the like. "Strangely," Kahn says, "that's not what the fight was focused on because we were plugging in to the larger community. [Many had the view that] a ferry linked to Foxwoods Casino should be opposed because gambling was sinful. That resulted in a lot of the support for Stop The Ferry... We didn't care where the support came from or why."

The legislation did not seek to restrict the current operations of the Viking Ferry—its operations to Block Island Sound and New London were pre-existing uses with no significant environmental or traffic impacts. However, it was obviously important that any expansion of the Viking Ferry operation be subjected to the same rules applicable to a new ferry service, and thus it was necessary to determine the existing passenger capacities of the ferries arriving and departing from the Viking terminal.

CCOM's January 1999 newsletter contained an update from President Bill Akin on the ferry situation.

> The Town Zoning Board of Appeals issued an absurd ruling granting the Viking Ferry a capacity of 1,927 daily departing passengers. CCOM has never had a problem with the Viking operation as we know it. As we know it means about 470 passengers—both coming and going—on a good day. The ZBA ruling was a surprise to everyone. The number was even higher than what Viking had asked for. Because we feel the possibility of a large-scale ferry

operation in Montauk poses a serious threat to Montauk's environment, CCOM has filed a lawsuit against the Town Zoning Board of Appeals.

The Town Board was also shocked by the Zoning Board ruling, and promptly amended the ferry legislation to spell out in unmistakable terms what it had intended in defining ferry passenger capacity.

The battle over ferries took four years before it was over. Except that it wasn't.

The Push to Stop Incorporation

Environmental threats have anything but a singular mode of unfolding. Rather, they often seem to surface all at once. Like the ferry threat, the issue of incorporation in Montauk arises again and again—and the issue is a divisive one. Some view the ferry and incorporation issues as not coincidentally connected.

There had been other attempts to push for incorporation, but it was in the mid-1990s that the movement significantly gathered force. In 1994, CCOM decided to join with the Committee to Stop Incorporation. According to Russell Stein, one of the underlying reasons behind the push for incorporation was that some business interests in the community wanted relief from zoning restrictions. CCOM's concerns related to zoning were environmental. In a letter to the editor of the *East Hampton Star* in October 1994, Rav Freidel warned, "should Montauk incorporate... we would [need to] start from scratch. The fact that many on the Committee to Incorporate Montauk are past violators of East Hampton zoning and other codes leads one to wonder what their real motive for incorporation is."

Freidel further explored the issue in a 1994 edition of the CCOM newsletter, getting at the complexities of the situation.

> Incorporation, is it good or bad? The answer is quite simply yes, it is both good and bad. The real question is, who is it good or bad for? There are some who, for very personal reasons, feel that the existing zoning regulations are 'draconian,' that they should be allowed to do with their property anything that they want, regard-

less of the impact it may have on their neighbors. Incorporation may serve these special interests well.

CCOM became an integral part of the Committee to Stop Incorporation and put money and membership effort on the line. Leading the committee were Judge James Ketcham and Bob Lamparter, of the Montauk Beach Property Owners Association (MBPOA), whose aim was to prove that incorporating Montauk would result in higher taxes and a loss of services, as well as endangering the protective zoning in place. CCOM earmarked $5,000 for the fight.

The incorporation vote was set for July 9, 1995. A letter went out the first week in June for voters, urging them to be in Montauk, as absentee ballots are not valid for incorporation votes, and a full-page ad with 500 names was prepared. The Committee to Stop Incorporation had found gross irregularities in the referendum petition. Word had it that the push for incorporation was being fueled by a view that a vote for it was a vote against CCOM—an unfortunate indication of the "us" and "them" climate in the hamlet.

The case against incorporation was buttressed by its price tag, which was costed out by Montauk resident Judge Ketcham with the help of Larry Cantwell, the East Hampton Village administrator. Cantwell showed how people in the village would be double and triple taxed.

Richard Kahn adds:

> The historic reason that villages were incorporated was to tighten up zoning because the Town zoning wasn't strong enough. Given who was promoting the incorporation movement [in Montauk], it was the opposite. We saw it was a way of getting Montauk to do its own zoning, and we knew which way that would turn out. The difficulty was that from CCOM's point of view: How do you fight Home Rule? Why shouldn't Montauk citizens control their own life?... We had to walk a little bit on eggs. Attacking it on financial grounds was the way to go, because nobody wanted to pay more taxes. The issue of zoning had to be raised delicately.

Ron Greenbaum, a former Town Supervisor, had been an advocate of incorporation, but after he met with Kahn and Joe Gaviola, president of the Montauk Harbor Association, to discuss the economic realities, he apparently saw the need to review the budgeting implications. Kahn recalls that when he and Greenbaum met with the incorporation group and talked about taxes, revenues, responsibilities, and indebtedness. "Ron Greenbaum tore away their budget," Kahn says.

Lisa Grenci recalls that 1996 was a turbulent time for East Hampton when she took office as president of CCOM. Certainly the move for incorporation was a contributing factor. The CCOM board was adamantly opposed to incorporation. "It was mostly based on not that we didn't want home rule, but that there was insecurity about the figures and documents and also the people who would be running the show," she says. "CCOM took a stand that we favored the right to vote by our community members [i.e., home rule], but we wouldn't support incorporation." Grenci resigned the CCOM presidency in 1997 to run for Town Council and was narrowly defeated.

Former board director Kay Dayton remarked, "We fought against it and those people are still trying to do it…. They were a group of mostly tradespeople. From their standpoint they didn't want to be restricted in any way. They didn't want any control from East Hampton and wanted to do what they pleased [when it came to zoning]."

Tom Ruhle says that incorporation was "the dumbest idea going. It might have made sense if they'd actually told the truth. There's no way you're going to create more government and it would cost less." It made no sense, he says, for the proponents of incorporation to insist that dismantling environmental laws would "cost less." Without regulation, the floodgates to further environmental abuse would be opened wide.

Montauk voters overwhelmingly defeated the incorporation attempt that year by 3-to-1 in a whopping turnout of 55% of registered voters. Of the 1,421 who turned out, 1,063 voted "no." Continuing the drama, the incorporation forces filed a challenge to the vote. Complaints were made against those who had challenged the petition signatures of the pro-incorporation referendum group. The suit was brought against Bob Lamparter, head of the anti-incorporation coalition; coordinator Maria Lubinska, a CCOM director; former director Robert Molnar; and Gloria Koza. Attorney Scott Allen was hired by the Committee to Stop Incorporation to deal with the challenge to the July

9th vote. The challenge was defeated, however, and the will of the majority of Montauk citizens prevailed.

Another drive to incorporate arose in 2004 (along with the attempt to introduce a high-speed, large-scale ferry to the Montauk area). "The movement seems to have picked up momentum with the Democrats' takeover of the Town Board in January," the *East Hampton Star* reported on March 11. The drive prompted more of the passionate, energetic activism that some in CCOM had seen as lessening. Clearly it had not.

Rumors had surfaced right after the elections that meetings for another incorporation plan were occurring, and that they were backed by former Town Supervisor Jay Schneiderman and former Town Budget Director Len Bernard. This new plan was said to include the downtown business district, certain motels, and the dock area, which would look like "a deformed octopus," according to an article in CCOM's January/February 2004 newsletter. The plan would have effectively excluded the majority of residential property owners from voting on the proposal. The idea—which would have allowed for Montauk's commercial sector to rewrite the zoning laws as they saw fit—was later abandoned. "It is unfortunate that, to our knowledge, no one from the incorporation organizing committee has approached the newly elected Town Board to discuss whatever grievances they may have," declared that CCOM newsletter. *New York Newsday* picked up on the issue on March 14, quoting Debra Foster, the Town Board member, responding to a frequently heard complaint by pro-incorporation advocate James Greenbaum, who claimed that the Town had "made it impossible for people to make modest improvements to their businesses and their homes." Foster pointed out that the problems could be resolved without separating from the Town. "That's a legitimate concern, and we would love their input," she said.

By mid-May, a highly polished brochure was sent to Montauk homeowners by the Committee for Montauk (whose membership was unknown), launching yet another attempt to remove Montauk from the stewardship of East Hampton Town. The CCOM newsletter that month headlined the issue: MONTAUK INCORPORATION: IDEALISM—OR A HIDDEN AGENDA? The article reported that "in comments to the *East Hampton Star*, the committee admitted that among their main concerns were personal past difficulties with the East Hampton Planning Department. A new village would put planning and zoning decisions in the hands of an elected Montauk Mayor and Board of Trustees."

By the end of May a questionnaire from the pro-incorporation group had been mailed to residents. It was viewed by many recipients as stacked in favor of incorporation. They felt it overlooked "what many consider to be the essence—and less commercial side—of Montauk's character" (according to the May/June 2004 CCOM newsletter). The brochure asked, "What event best represents the essence of Montauk?" and went on to list, among other things, the St. Patrick's Day parade and the Blessing of the Fleet. It made no mention whatsoever of anything to do with open space, beaches, or even the opportunity to enjoy Montauk's unique environment. It sounded just like what it was, a Chamber of Commerce PR piece.

On July 3, the CCOM board met and unanimously voted their opposition to the incorporation of Montauk as a separate village. That announcement was included in a July 9 press release, which was picked up and incorporated into an article which ran in the July 11 edition of the Sunday *New York Times* just prior to the informational meeting called by the pro-incorporation group for that day. In the press release CCOM President Bill Akin wrote, "The underlying issue is control of the planning and zoning process. Incorporation would lead to the accelerated commercialization of Montauk at the expense of the environment, its year-round residents and, ultimately, our tourist economy which is dependent upon environmental preservation."

The pro-incorporation meeting at the Montauk Firehouse on that Sunday, July 11, brought out a huge crowd and included a vociferous contingent of the Montauk Beach Property Owners Association as well as CCOM members. And, for the first time, some of the pro-incorporation members made themselves known. With the exception of one local doctor, the group consisted primarily of real estate brokers, motel owners, and downtown business owners. William Esseks had been hired as the group's attorney and was also present. Many in the audience objected to the structure of the meeting, which initially allowed for little if any commentary or questioning while a survey and budget matters were presented.

Following the meeting, efforts were made by Bill Akin to meet with the pro-incorporation leaders and hash out their differences. Nevertheless, "with discussion on differences hitting a wall last Thursday night," wrote the July 21 issue of the *East Hampton Independent*, "the Concerned Citizens of Montauk moved forward the next morning with a press conference rebutting aspects of a proposed incorporation… Akin offered a 13-point presentation entitled 'What you should really know about incorporation.'"

1. A vote to incorporate is a very serious decision.

As an incorporated village Montauk will no longer be bound to follow the zoning or planning laws and recommendations determined by the government of East Hampton.

2. The budget for an incorporated village is set by the Village Board consisting of a Mayor and four Trustees.

Comparisons to other village budgets are merely speculation about what might be, but by no means will be. [Akin commented that the voting on incorporation would not be on a budget, but on a legal entity.]

3. A Montauk Village would continue to pay taxes to the Town of East Hampton.

By becoming a village, Montauk would be adding another layer of government… a new village would become an additional line on everyone's annual tax bill.

4. The committee proposing Montauk become an incorporated village consists almost entirely of individuals with business or development interests in Montauk.

5. "Home Rule" and "Autonomy" are two pleasant-sounding, but meaningless words the incorporation committee uses to promote the idea for incorporating Montauk as a village. The fact is Montauk has been very well served as part of the Township of East Hampton.

6. The Planning Department contemplated by the proposed village budget would not have any full-time planners and could not reasonably be expected to perform its duties.

7. The proposed Building Department and Code Office for the new village would be clearly inadequate.

8. Purchasers of property in a Montauk Village would still be required to pay into the Community Preservation Fund (CPF) but the Town would have no obligation to spend any of the CPF funds for acquisition of land in the new Village.

9. Montauk's Fire Department has been a model for other towns for decades, but under incorporation it would lose its autonomy.

10. Property owners in Hither Hills (Montauk Beach Property Owners Association) would lose their deeds to the beach access property in front of their homes.

11. If Montauk were to be incorporated, who will run for the office of Mayor and Village Trustee? And who will run for office in 10 years? While technically any registered voter can run for office, most villages where the elected official must volunteer to serve for little or no salary (as has been proposed for Montauk), the majority of positions are held by local business people.... It is possible, if not highly likely, that over time Montauk's government would be made up of citizens who have a vested interest in promoting commercial interests over those of other home owners and seasonal residents.

12. Over the almost universal objection of Montauk residents some members of the incorporation committee continue to suggest that passenger ferry service from Connecticut to the South Fork would be beneficial.

13. By becoming a village, Montauk risks introducing what has almost everywhere else become bitter political hostilities into this community.

"Stay tuned," the CCOM newsletter warned.

I WANT YOU TO PARTY

★ SAT. JULY 1ˢᵗ 5-7:30 PM ★ DEEP HOLLOW RANCH ★
$25 TAX-DEDUCTIBLE DONATION ★ BENEFITS THE MONTAUK ENVIRONMENT.
Concerned Citizens Of Montauk

Chapter 6

Saved Is Never Secure: Montauk at the 21st Century

I T IS OBVIOUS THAT INCORPORATION and an expanded ferry service are issues which never seem to be fully resolved—but they are not the only ongoing, long-term concerns of CCOM. Environmental issues are never really wrapped up neatly to everyone's satisfaction, either. Even when activism causes laws to be passed, regulations to be tightened, or simply raises the awareness of citizens, continuing preservation requires constant vigilance. Much of Montauk's environment has been safeguarded—but much remains to be done. As CCOM moves into the new century, these are some of the new concerns the organization faces.

County Park (Indian Field)

Acquisition of open space is one part of the environmental quotient, while protection, through wise stewardship, is the other. This applies to Montauk County Park (now called Theodore Roosevelt County Park), the land that started it all for CCOM: the place where Hilda Lindley fought to prevent 1,400 homes, as well as a new inlet and

From the highest point in Theodore Roosevelt County Park, the view includes Oyster Pond and Montauk Point State Park.

marinas, from destroying the natural freshwater ecosystem. The rolling hills are still home to fox, deer, hundreds of bird species, and flora. As a park, the eco-friendly trail system welcomes the adventurous tourist and provides wilderness solitude for winter locals and hunters. Known for many years as Third House County Park (named after the headquarters building that was once called the "third shepherd's house" during the cattle-grazing centuries), the park stretches from Route 27 north to Oyster Pond and Shagwong Point, and west until it crests the ridge of hills now home to a multitude of summer houses accessed from East Lake Drive.

In March of 1990, CCOM discovered that Third House, its cottages, and other buildings in the park were to be licensed for commercial use as a restaurant, bar, and guest accommodations. The individual who held the county franchise for the Deep Hollow Stables had invited architects, engineers, and electricians to look over Third House. When called by CCOM, County Legislator Fred Thiele was unaware of this project, although Richard White Jr. of Montauk, a trustee on the County Park Commission, was aware of it and expressed approval. Richard Finn, acting park commissioner at the time, assured Thiele there was "nothing on paper."

Finn later acknowledged that he was in fact working on such a plan, but he wouldn't say much about it. He did admit that private use of the park property would have to go out for bidding. CCOM immediately challenged the availability of potable water for a restaurant. Finn didn't view a State Environmental Quality Review Act (SEQRA) review as necessary, but CCOM maintained that this was a requirement. Finn's request for proposals finally became available on May 17 and called for bids to be returned May 31—an impossible schedule for bidders to meet.

Then-County Legislator Fred Thiele was furious to learn of this proposal in a County Park within his district. He introduced a resolution calling for a moratorium until the County Parks Department could prepare a management plan for the park. CCOM and others spoke before the County Legislature in support of this resolution. CCOM members were urged to write speedily in support, because the privatization of Third House and its loss to the public was scheduled to become effective on July 1, 1990.

The public outcry to the first proposed plan was so vociferous that newly elected County Legislator Bill Jones sent the plan back to the drawing board. An advisory committee was formed; CCOM's Veronica Garvey was named a member. The group met biweekly over more than three years, investigating every aspect of the park. They gave audience to all ideas and interested parties to develop appropriate uses for the park. Three years later, a comprehensive plan for the preservation of Montauk County Park was released. Its goals were to:

1. Develop environmental and interpretive programs, both environmental and historical.

2. Develop active recreational programs, including the improvement and expansion of the trails system; maintain camping, hunting, [and] riding in a way that protects sensitive environmental features.

CCOM contributed $10,000 from 2003 to 2004 to the construction of the new greenhouse at Montauk Public School.

CCOM AND KIDS

In 1997, CCOM President Lisa Grenci involved two young teachers at the local school, Chantal Adamcewicz and Rachel Kleinberg, in forming an after-school club called the Concerned Students of Montauk (CSOM). The club was formed to help the children become more aware of local environmental issues through research, discussion, and field trips. Subsequent to the club's founding, CCOM's Earth Day event has involved a litter cleanup, with the children participating.

CCOM continued its connection with the school by donating $10,000 to the school's greenhouse, which had become dilapidated. A new greenhouse was completed and dedicated in the spring of 2005.

Carol Morrison, former president and ongoing director of CCOM, spearheaded the formation of a Nature Center at Theodore Roosevelt Country Park's Third House. With financial aid from CCOM and private citizens, the Center runs programs primarily for children year-round, including hikes, lectures, and other events. These efforts, combined with the previously mentioned Field Day, demonstrate that CCOM's view of Montauk's future includes every generation.

3. Rehabilitate the Third House complex—to be an integrated combination of a visitors' center, environmental educational center, the Pharaoh museum center/living museum, Theodore Roosevelt room/display, wildlife rehabilitation center, [and] snack bar/trading post.

4. Manage the ecological features of the park to restore the species composition, biodiversity, and functioning of the many ecosystems in the par.

5. Enhance the aesthetic experience of the park through better access to scenic vistas.

CCOM called the plan a "marvel of balance." The plan went to the County Legislature on September 17, 1995 and was unanimously adopted in 1996. Announcing the news, the CCOM's newsletter states: "Once the plans are put into effect, Montauk County Park will truly be what the plan envisions, a jewel in the county park system."

Most recently, in 2005, Third House is undergoing renovations. Plans for use are somewhat uncertain, but CCOM continues as a watchdog to guard against overcommercialization.

Turtle Cove

In 1981 the federal government deeded 17.4 acres of beachfront known as Turtle Cove to the Town of East Hampton. They mistakenly thought this would make everyone happy. The cove lies in the shadow of the Montauk lighthouse and has been known for generations as a prime surfcasting and surfing location. Under the terms of the transfer agreement, the land was to be used only for passive recreation and "controlled access" to ocean fishing. Just a few hundred yards from Turtle Cove are the two biggest parking lots east of the Shinnecock Canal. Built to service the crowds coming to tour the lighthouse, these parking lots have been used for decades by surfers and surfcasters as well. After leaving their cars and trucks in the lots, they would easily walk down a very well-maintained trail to the cove beach.

Problems started after a utility road used to bring in stones for the lighthouse revetment was left open in the 1990s. All of a sudden, Turtle

Turtle Cove, as seen from the top of the Montauk Lighthouse, lies just east of Camp Hero where the old radar tower stands in contrast to the preserved wilderness.

Cove's limited beach was overwhelmed with trucks and SUVs. Declared an outraged Rav Freidel, "Here we have two giant parking lots 500 yards away, and people can't walk down to Turtle Cove. They have to drive. It defies comprehension."

Battle lines swiftly formed: CCOM, the Surfriders Foundation, and the East Hampton Trails Preservation Society on one side (park and walk), and the other side (cars on the beach). The Town was stuck in the middle. But because it was obvious that the land was not being used in accordance with the original intent, Elyse LaForest of the Federal Lands to Parks Program instructed the Town to devise an acceptable management plan—or the National Parks Service would retake the land. In 2003, the Town came up with an eleventh-hour plan that satisfied nobody, including LaForest. The plan allowed 24 cars to park down at the cove for the popular fall fishing season. A gate was installed at the top of the access road to keep traffic off the beach at other times. This very substantial steel gate had been up for only three

The view of the ocean as seen coming into Montauk would have been blocked by condos if CCOM hadn't taken the lead in pulling other organizations together to urge the Town to purchase this small but crucial parcel.

days when it was cut down and deposited in the ocean. Everybody knew who did it, but nobody wanted to accuse anybody publicly.

A new Town administration inherited the problem in 2004, but has not yet come up with any workable solution.

The Open Space Plan

Though a large focus of the CCOM had been on the preservation of large tracts of land, much of what was possible to be protected had been acquired by the year 2000. The group began turning its attention to the acquisition of small lots in Montauk. CCOM's newsletter in December of 2000, stated:

> It's been a good year for the Good Guys. Shadmoor was saved. That alone makes it a good year. But other open space parcels taken off the market in 2000 also deserve a Christmas greeting: 95 acres

between Fort Pond Bay and Hither Woods, 117 acres across Flamingo from Culloden Point, 30 acres purchased by the town
around Stepping Stone Pond, and 53 acres of wetlands donated to
the town by 511 Equities.

This positive gain for the Montauk community came as a result of a
Town open space plan that had a significant focus on Montauk. The
previous open space plan of 1995 had warned of threatening levels of
development in the hamlet that could increase by as much as 50 percent. The new plan was reviewed at a public hearing on March 15,
1996, and was to be later incorporated into the Town's comprehensive
plan. CCOM was actively promoting the open space plan, urging Montauk's residents to attend the hearing. The new plan contained "an
exhaustive inventory of all open space from Wainscott to Montauk,
plus recommendations for 700 specific parcels."

CCOM board member Lisa Grenci was appointed a member of the
Town's newly created Open Space Advisory Committee in 1996. The
group's mission was to help the Town prioritize land to be preserved.
In 2001, CCOM supported a bipartisan proposal authorizing the Town
to borrow $5 million to purchase small lots for neighborhood open
space and parks. The purpose was to put together groupings of small
lots to create trail linkages and to reduce density in developed areas.
The proposal was successful.

Coming into the 21st century, saving open space was a priority for
many, not only CCOM. One parcel that benefited from the public's support of open space acquisition was the small, but critical, parcel everyone sees coming into town. Having become friends with Panoramic
View's owner, John French, CCOM President Bill Akin recalls:

> I didn't know it but the French family owned that piece of empty
> property that you see first thing when you come into town,
> between the Oceanside Motel and the parking lot for the beach
> there. John called me and said, "Boy, it doesn't look like there's
> anything I can do. Five family members who live in Nebraska, Col-
> orado and other places called me. They want their money out and
> we're going to have to sell it."... John had two if not three valid

bids for that property to build what would have amounted to four or five condominium units, upside down units.... We would have lost that view [of the dunes and ocean] when you first drive into Montauk.... I think that would have been extremely disturbing.

Akin called Jay Schneiderman, Town Supervisor at the time, informing him that the property was not on the Community Preservation Fund list and relating his concerns about losing it. He then called Gail Webb and Jan McKeon of the Montauk Village Association, which managed Kirk Park across the street. He also contacted Dick White, Jr. of the Historical Society. None of those contacted wanted the property to be sold. "So I called Jay and said, 'Listen, there isn't an organization in this Town that wants to see that built up,'" Akin recalls. Schneiderman took the matter to the Town Board and they bought the property. "They bought it in such a way that it can have some recreational purposes or some low-impact uses... but the skyline is preserved," Akin says.

In 2000 the Town embarked on developing a new Comprehensive Plan. With many board members serving on committees advising on the plan, CCOM was able to make a strong case for open space, both large- and small-acquisition.

CCOM's concerns were presented in a front-page article in the CCOM newsletter of January 2003. "We must emphasize to the consult-ants [Horne Rose] that increased density in some parts of town—for instance, in creating desperately needed affordable housing—must be compensated by a reduction of permitted density elsewhere," the newsletter stated. "Open space acquisition of both big and small lots must be a priority."

The need to restrict tear-downs, to control and maintain building scale, and to retain the "nonconforming use" limitation were spelled out in the article. Some see this as too restrictive, but CCOM's view is that upholding it is critical to maintaining the character of neighbor-hoods. The newsletter article discussed other key concerns as well: groundwater and surface water quality, and the need for an aquifer-pro-tection plan, a watershed-management plan, and a harbor-management plan. Code enforcement and all other aspects of development that threaten the quality of life were imperatives. Reminding members that, in preparing to launch the new comprehensive plan, the Town had sent a questionnaire to 17,000 residents and that with an outstanding 25% rate of return, the first priority of the respondents was maintaining the rural character of East Hampton by restricting growth, the piece ended with a plea to members as the Comprehensive Plan was moving into its final stages of work. "Please make your voice heard!" the newsletter implored. A completed comprehensive plan was approved by the East Hampton Town Board on May 6, 2005. It is hoped that it will help to sustain the rural quality of life in Montauk.

Camp Hero

Although the Camp Hero land had been successfully purchased in the 1980s, a new kind of threat surfaced more than 10 years later. Bernadette Castro, the New York State Commissioner of Parks, Recreation and Historic Preservation, wanted to develop a golf course there. When the state applied to the federal government in 1984 for acquisition of the property as part of the park system, they had promised to maintain it as a park preserve, a status which mandates only "passive recreation," which includes activities such as hiking, fishing, picnicking, and bird-watching. But Mike Bottini, a planner with the Group for the South Fork, was a guest at the January 1996 CCOM board meeting, and arrived with a large map of Camp Hero Park. He explained that the land had never officially been put into preserve status, and therefore didn't carry the strict mandates which CCOM had assumed were in place.

Though the Department of the Interior had ruled after a two-year fight that a golf course would not be consistent with the use for which the land had been transferred as part of the Federal Lands to Parks program, Rav Freidel was concerned that this ruling could be overturned. Freidel, who had passionately fought to obtain the acreage, wrote letters to Castro and other officials on behalf of CCOM. He described this environmentally sensitive land, which contains endangered species, significant wetlands, and rare strands of the Montauk Moorlands. Freidel delineated the environmental impacts posed by a golf course, including the effects of herbicides and pesticides and the limited water

BERNADETTE CASTRO, commissioner of the State Parks, Recreation, and Historic Preservation Department, welcomed the public to Camp Hero State Park yesterday. The cold war-era radar tower, which could detect airborne objects more than 200 miles away, will be preserved. *Morgan McGivern*

Camp Hero State Park Opens

Despite CCOM's successful efforts to prevent Camp Hero from being sold to private developers in 1984, the group was not mentioned at the dedication ceremony, nor were they invited to attend.

available. "We intend to oppose construction of a golf course at Camp Hero," he wrote, but also expressed CCOM's willingness to participate in a citizens advisory committee on park utilization for passive recreation. "This land shouldn't be looked at as a cash cow," he concluded. "Some other things are more important in life than doing what would irrevocably damage our natural gifts."

In December of 1997, Judge James Ketcham showed the CCOM board a video about the movement to privatize national parks. Put out by the National Parks Conservation Authority (NPCA), the video demonstrated that the pressures in Montauk to privatize parks were part of a national trend. Following up on this at the meeting, Rav Freidel reported that the effort to get Camp Hero into Preserve status was being stalemated by the head of the Philadelphia office of the National Park Service. Something was terribly amiss.

Why, of all things, a golf course? Freidel offers background. Castro had brought in Ed Wankel as Commissioner of Parks for Suffolk

County. Wankel was a golfer, and he did a study to look at the possibilities of developing more golf courses in Suffolk County. "He got golf in Castro's ear, and the state sent out a 'request for proposals' to build a 250-acre champion golf course at Camp Hero. Once again, we thought the property was saved, and you're in a fight again," Freidel says.

Over time, Freidel noted, golf courses use 10 times the amount of herbicides and pesticides than farms use. The minutes of CCOM's meeting of March 2, 1996 reflect that "there was no advisory committee to the golf course established, and no information turned over," CCOM sent a Freedom of Information Request to the state regarding Camp Hero. Two months after receiving no response, Richard Kahn wrote a follow-up letter. CCOM received no response for six months. "They were playing hardball and violating the law by not responding promptly to the request," said Freidel. CCOM sent a letter to Castro providing information regarding the migrations of hundreds of thousands of birds who use Camp Hero as a rest stop along the Great Eastern Flyway. They pointed out that "every one of the plants out there produces a kind of berry that feeds another kind of bird... mowing it down into a lawn and chasing a white ball where the only birdies were going to be somebody shooting one under par, as opposed to what we have here, was quite destructive and troubling."

"We were interested in the water study they did on Camp Hero [which stated that] there was plenty of water for a golf course," Freidel continues. It took four requests to get the information from the state. It was an inadequate study, a mere few pages long and nary a test well drilled. When CCOM finally obtained it, Freidel says, "the state had redacted with a black magic marker more than half of the water study. You couldn't read a word!" It was censored to the public. The only thing not blocked out was the part of the study saying there was enough water.

John Kelley, regional director of the Federal Parks Program, called Freidel and asked whether the state had contacted him about its plans for Camp Hero. When Freidel replied in the negative, Kelley informed him that the state was required to get input from all the groups involved in the original acquisition—that is, the National Park Service had a say about the use of the property. U.S. PARK SERVICE OPPOSES CAMP

Camp Hero State Park in the winter.

HERO GOLF COURSE, ran the CCOM newsletter headline in March 1996. The article exultantly declared that "the National Park Service refused to allow the state to change the utilization of the 450-acre parcel from passive to active use."

"Castro got a lot of heat," declared Freidel. "There were tremendous amounts of people contacted." He credits Richard Kahn's assistance in drafting much of the correspondence. Freidel goes on,

> An awful lot of people were applying pressure. Some included: the GSF, Nature Conservancy, National Audubon Society, Congressman Forbes, Assemblymen Thiele and Englebright and Senator Moynihan. Friends of mine high up in the Republican Party upstate would meet Castro on other issues and, doing the favor for me, would raise the issue of the golf course. By the by, Ed Wankel was fired. Castro got rid of him and got rid of the plans to build a golf course. (He took the fall for her.) There was an awful lot of controversy over it, something she didn't want.

Larry Penny, as head of the Town's Natural Resource Department, was strongly against Castro's golf course plan. He spent considerable time at Camp Hero with planner Lisa Liquori, who also knew the property well; both were aware of how inappropriate the plan was. "I think Bernadette [Castro] knew that it never was going to happen," Penny remembers. In the summer of 1999, Bernadette Castro met with members of the Camp Hero Advisory Committee. The most significant news coming out of the meeting—and hailed by CCOM—was her statement that "golf is no longer an option for this property."

Kahn points out the lesson derived regarding environmental wars:

> Even when you do get land preservation, it doesn't mean you're home free. Bernadette Castro could never understand why we're not making a profit out of our state parks. Why don't we convert one of the last unique remaining maritime oak and holly forests into a championship golf course? That got chopped down, mostly by CCOM.... So all along it's been an issue of not only obtaining the property, but also protecting it.

His position can be well underscored by a CCOM's front-page newsletter headline in January 1997: CCOM TO N.Y.S.: "LEAVE OUR PARKS ALONE." The story included not only the state's interest in Camp Hero becoming "the Pebble Beach of the East," to quote Bill Akin, but a possible study of the feasibility of a golf course in Hither Woods, the sole-source aquifer protecting Montauk's water supply. According to Richard Kahn and Rav Freidel, they had seen a map of a planned golf course for Hither Woods in the Park Commission's office in Bethpage. Fortunately—and possibly because of the outcome of the Camp Hero golf fiasco—it never materialized.

The state finally decided to gather a citizens advisory group, and the National Park Service called Rav Freidel to ask for recommendations of group members. "We gave them a list, they gave it to the state, and the state left off half of them," reports an incredulous Freidel. "It took three or four days before... I learned people were left out. I called John Kelley and he reamed out the state. We were able to get the Long Island Botanical Society, Audubon Society, Jim Ash from the South Fork Natural History Society [on the advisory group]. We got people at the last minute, but even then the state was trying to pull a fast one [involving] some group nobody ever heard of called Montauk Residents for Golf."

It was a protracted struggle. The organization also had to keep a watchful eye on the Army Corps of Engineers and their clean-up program for the site (to remove ordnance from an area used by the Army during World War II). Then the advisory committee was confronted with a new wrinkle: Castro's consideration of another commercial revenue source, the construction of 18 cabins for rental as camping accommodations. Lisa Grenci, who attended the meeting, quoted Castro to the board as saying that she "gave in on the golf course issue so we [advisory committee] shouldn't fight the cabins."

CCOM board members expressed dismay for this plan, both because of water and septic issues and because of opposition to the privatization of state parks. The board was also skeptical that the state would limit the plan to 18 cabins if its goal was to produce revenue in excess of costs. That plan was also challenged by the Montauk Chamber of Commerce, which conveyed a clear message that there were already adequate motel rooms in Montauk. The opposition was effective, and the plan didn't take.

Code Enforcement

There are other items on CCOM's "unfinished business" list in addition to issues of land preservation. With various environmental threats continually in play—and often conflicting with the interests of local Montauk business and property owners—the issue of code enforcement is another area where constant vigilance is required.

The Crows' Nest is a restaurant located in a residential area. An old, seedy restaurant bordering marshland on the west side of Lake Montauk, it has long been a local hangout. The business has thwarted many ordinances over the years, yet it continues to obtain permits for mass gatherings. This dramatic kind of overusage creates dead zones in the lake, like "Peter's Run" by the Anchorage Inn. When someone takes a small mom-and-pop restaurant located in a residential area and starts catering 15 summer weekend weddings with outdoor DJs playing music until 1:00 AM and the Town doesn't think there is a problem—

Former President Dorothy Disken (left) and current President Bill Akin (right) at a recent Board meeting.

well, that's the problem. The Crow's Nest is just one of many examples where the lack of effective code enforcement began to erode the quality of life in Montauk in the 1990s as more and more people poured in on summer weekends. Noise, intrusive lighting, overcrowded housing, and poor parking facilities all combined to overwhelm a short-staffed, poorly trained, and often legally restrained code enforcement department. Worse, the courts seemed to have little inclination to back up whatever limited enforcement there was.

"They took a 'mom and pop' operation and changed it to a wedding business," Richard Kahn says. "Over 20 convictions over the years, [and] the courts give them a slap on the wrist... The way to go after this is to write them up every day and then they'd have multiple violations. Then the judges [who have said their powers are limited] could do something. But the Town hems and haws." He acknowledges that the situation is improving somewhat, with the increase in code enforcement officers.

"It was all politically driven," states Kahn. He provides another example:

The Anchorage restaurant on West Lake Drive was about to fail (in about 1990). They started with live bands—the noise, the lights; people spilling out at 4 o'clock in the morning screaming. All in a residential neighborhood. We tried to get the Town to do something, but they were just "too busy" and, of course, the code enforcement officers don't work at night.

Fortunately, Tom Ruhle was a councilman. One night some of the drunks spilled out and crossed the street and set on fire... Tommy Ruhle's mother's bathing suit that was hanging on the line.... So Tommy's mother said, "Tommy, that's not allowed. Put an end to this place." The next thing you know, the cops were there; not inside, but what they would do is stop every car leaving the Anchorage and check for alcohol. That word took about two weeks to get around, and that was the end of the Anchorage, because of Tommy Ruhle's mother's bathing suit!

Shepherd's Neck Inn, which dates back to the 1930s, is another long-term problematic structure. Overbuilt, having added 23 units with bathrooms without obtaining permits and without adequate parking facilities, the business was operating without a certificate of occupancy. The property was put up for sale and was located adjacent to an affordable housing district next to Fort Pond. Eventually the Town realized that putting that district there was not a good idea, as the septic waste provisions couldn't handle the density. Word on the street then circulated that "a quiet deal" had been agreed to. The deal was that in exchange for giving up the affordable housing overlay, the Town would rezone the area from residential to commercial. This would allow the inn to provide for parking in accordance with the planning department's rules. This deal would be a major step towards legalizing the 23 illegal units.

CCOM was not pleased with the message that a flagrant code violator would be bailed out by rezoning his property, and were concerned that the transient hotel could be converted into permanent housing. The organization has been seeking assurances from the Town that this will not occur. "Not that we don't need affordable housing in Montauk," acknowledges Richard Kahn, "but to convert this when there are no kitchen facilities and no laundry facilities is inhuman." Slowly, very slowly, the Town has been making progress by beefing up the Code Enforcement Department and ensuring more vigorous prosecution of scofflaws, but the process has not been easy. Too often simple violations, for example outdoor storefront displays, get targeted while issues like noise pollution, overcrowding, and intrusive lighting that affect far more people get a lot of talk, but very little walk.

The Ferry Threat: 2005 and Running

In March of 2004, a group of planners from the New York Metropolitan Transportation Council, the Greater Bridgeport Regional Planning Agency, and the Southwestern Regional Planning Agency of Connecticut held a meeting in Southold (on the North Fork of Long Island) to explain their plans for ferry service from Connecticut. Various ports on Long Island, including two locations in Montauk and one in Napeague, were under consideration. The problem was that these apparently intelligent and well-qualified planners never bothered to speak to any citizen or governmental representative from the Town of East Hampton.

As a result, CCOM hired a bus, filled it with protesters, and drove to the Southold meeting. In an unprecedented step, every member of the East Hampton Town Board also came to the meeting.

FEAR FORCED FERRIES, ran the headline in the *East Hampton Star* on March 23. Town Councilwoman Debra Foster was quoted as saying, "Danger. Danger. Danger," to her Town Board colleagues, and the article summarized her view that "the proposal could mean up to three ferries landing in Montauk." The proposal's map showed possible ferry landing sites at Lake Montauk, Fort Pond Bay, and the former fish factory in Napeague Bay.

Pete Hammerle was most clear when he said: "It's simple: Color us red" (meaning not an option). The opposition was heard and the planners withdrew to "take a second look at the Montauk locations." Then in late 2004, the heavy artillery was unveiled. The Towns of Southold and Shelter Island—having completely mismanaged their own traffic planning—joined with the Cross Sound Ferry Company to file a lawsuit against the Town of East Hampton asking the court to declare the East Hampton law governing ferry terminals and high-speed ferries invalid.

Southold, and to a lesser extent Shelter Island, never anticipated the avalanche of cars racing to deliver their occupants onto the high-speed ferries operating in conjunction with two new Connecticut gambling casinos. The result has been a traffic nightmare for local residents, particularly those with driveways on Route 25 east of Greenport. While only a small fraction of the cars originate from the Town of East Hampton, Southold and Shelter Island politicians, eager to shift the blame away from their own shortsighted decisions, are trying to sell a Montauk ferry route as a solution to their self-imposed problems.

East Hampton officials are confident that the law will be upheld. The Town has hired top environmental lawyer Michael Gerrard, who was instrumental advising the earlier Stop the Ferry committee, and Southampton lawyer Richard Cahn, to defend its interests. Most recently, in March of 2005, to the surprise and consternation of many, the Viking Ferry, operated by the local Forsberg family, filed a separate suit against East Hampton seeking to overturn the Town's ferry legislation.

As this book goes to press these two lawsuits represent the biggest threat to the existence of Montauk as people know it. There is no doubt that fast passenger ferry service to and from New London, as well as car ferry service, would have a major negative impact on the environment, the already serious traffic problem, and the overall quality of life. It would be the end of The End.

Behind the Headlines

While land acquisition battles and lawsuits aimed at protecting Montauk's environment generated most of the headlines for CCOM, it was the continual lineup of local events and community service presentations that personalized the organization. Right from the start Hilda Lindley insisted CCOM sponsor presentations open to the public on topics that were important to the Montauk environment. And she insisted on a good party every now and then.

Probably the most recognized of any CCOM function has been the

Everyone joins in to clean up Montauk during CCOM's annual Earth Day litter pick-up (2003).

annual Meet The Candidates forum. For 35 years straight CCOM has hosted a very well attended and locally televised forum in late October where local, county, state, and federal candidates could explain their positions to the audience, and the audience could in turn ask questions. Most recently hosted by Peter Lowenstein and Dr. Martin Post, Meet The Candidates has provided an invaluable opportunity for local voters to meet face to face with congressmen, senators, as well as the state and local representatives who make the decisions that impact our lives every day.

For most of CCOM's history the person who was most identified locally with the organization was Kay Carley. A founding board member,

Some CCOM festivities (from top): Earth Day (2003), annual New Years Day celebration (1997), fun and games: a potato sack race and pie throw at Field Day (2004).

Founding board member Kay Carley organized CCOM's annual raffle for decades.

for decades Kay ran the annual CCOM raffle which was an important source of financial support for the organization. Every year Kay would gather more than 100 prizes donated by local businesses. Then she and other board members, rain or shine, would sit in front of the post office selling raffle tickets. It was a thankless job, but a typical example of the commitment many CCOM members have shown over the years.

Throughout every season of the year CCOM interacts with the community in some way. In summer the CCOM gala served as a fun low-key rally for the membership and anyone who wanted to attend. It took the voluntary help of more than 20 CCOM members to pull it off every year.

The fall has always been CCOM busiest season. Every year at CCOM's Annual Meeting one or more speakers are invited to addresses some issue important to Montauk. And the public has always been invited. Beach erosion, open space acquisition, code enforcement, light pollution, and the potential for catastrophic hurricane damage are only a few of the most recent topics. The Annual Meeting is then followed by Meet The Candidates in October.

On New Years Day it has been a long CCOM tradition to have a beach party. Open to anyone who wanted to come, CCOM members including Maria Lubinska and Dick "Raw-Chicken" Johnson, year after year have prepared memorable cold weather picnic fare. (Maria's soup was truly spectacular.)

In April the organization kicks off the year with an Earth Day celebration that in recent years has centered around a roadside and beach clean up. With help from Julie Marcley and the Montauk Litter Task Force, the clean up, followed by hot dogs and entertainment at Kirk Park or the Montauk Public School, has been both successful and fun. With kids, parents and even a few dogs participating, over 100 bags of litter as well as a few tires, mattresses, washing machines, abandoned bicycles, and always at least one still unopened bottle of vodka are cleaned from Montauk roads and beaches.

The newest and by far the biggest CCOM event is Field Day. Combining forces with the amazing group of local moms who run Montauk Youth, the two organizations have renewed an old Montauk fall celebration devoted exclusively to kids. For the last three years more than 300 boys, girls, moms, dads, and CCOM members have come together at the County Park to just have fun. Old fashion potato sack races, fair ground games, a bubble gum bubble blowing contest and of course a pie-throwing event have turned this into a must for the local families.

Putting on all these events takes substantial planning, a financial commitment, and plain old hard work. While every CCOM board member has at one time or another helped out, lately the organization has developed a team of event specialists that have managed all the outdoor events. The core of the team consists of Gene Wolsk, Ray Cortell, Peter Lowenstein, Eugene White, Jean Fisher, and Mike Mahoney. And as always, local Montauk businesses have been extremely generous in donating food, beverages, and prizes whenever they are asked. They never fail to demonstrate how the whole community is committed to the Montauk environment.

Sometimes it takes something other than an event to make a difference in the community. In 2003, the Montauk Public School recognized that their greenhouse could not be repaired and had to be replaced. CCOM stepped up and donated $10,000 to help make the project possible. Local builder Dan Stavola donated material and labor and by 2005 the job was done. The school had a whole new greenhouse. This kind of thing happens again and again in Montauk, proving that it's the people as well as the place that make it special.

Finally, whether it's raising money, mailing out thousands of envelopes, or digging through file after file in some obscure Town office, none of CCOM's work would be possible without the work of people like Jodi Grindrod, CCOM's technical associate who does double duty working for the Group For The South Fork, or Shirley Katz, CCOM Treasurer since 1997, Céline Keating who writes and edits the quarterly newsletter, past Treasurer and Chairperson of the nominating committee Veronica Garvey, and the tireless Rita McKernan who has managed CCOM's membership records since day one 35 years ago. Inside the wrapper of headlines and photo ops, these are the people who make CCOM work.

Conclusion: Saved Is Never Secure

It is evident that the efforts of CCOM's work will never be finished. But, having worked successfully to preserve many large and small properties, some may question whether the mission of the organization is still the same. To that point, several members of the community and of CCOM were asked for their views on the current or future focus for the organization.

Rav Freidel feels that there is much that still has to be done in terms of the water. He is pleased that CCOM has expanded its horizons in terms of water protection, conveying the message that "if you want to protect Montauk and keep it from getting carved up, then you've got to protect the water quality of the region and have sustainable fisheries."

Says Larry Penny:

If I had my druthers, I would like to see CCOM work to have a [marine] sanctuary off Montauk. I would like to see the Outer Lands Sanctuary... It would extend from Block Island to Nantucket. Maybe the commercial fishermen would have a hard time with that, until they realized that the sanctuary would be a habitat and the fish would come back. Right now they are going to fish themselves into nothing. I'd like to see us have a Fisheries Department to support the fishermen, while practicing good conservation.

Carol Morrison says, "We've done the big things... I think we've proved that open space is cheaper than development." She believes that the fighting objective for CCOM now is about code enforcement. "Quality of Life is the new, big slogan." Founder Rita McKernan agrees, saying that she "would like to see code enforcement as a priority. Some people get away with a lot."

Both Dorothy and Lillian Disken feel that the highest priority for CCOM needs to be about groundwater, especially considering the increased population.

Says Tom Ruhle:

> For the longest time the battle was on preserving open space. At some time we're going to have to deal with the occupied land, the quality of life, of the environment. You don't load your lot up with chemicals that kill anything that moves. CCOM has done and needs to continue its program to educate people to clean up and protect the ground we have.

Ruhle is not unmindful of the effects of the work the organization has achieved. But there is a downside. "The irony is that the better job you do to preserve the community, the more people want to live here." He is troubled by the large, looming structures that are changing the visual landscape in Montauk. "We used to have summer cottages—cute and beachy, small houses, small neighborhood, everything to scale. That's the next battle, looking at the neighborhood and trying to preserve those areas." He adds that the biggest challenge Montauk will face is that because of the preservation efforts, "it's going to be the most attractive place to live on Long Island."

Aside from the constant concerns about ground water, Kay Dayton sees increasing threats to the land that has already been preserved.

My feeling is that given the nature of people, there's always going

THE NEW YORK TIMES, SUNDAY, AUGUST 16, 1992

In the Region: **Long Island**

Montauk Park Refurbishing Stirs Debate

Preservationists Angry Over Plans For Concession

By DIANA SHAMAN

TWO years ago, the State Legislature directed Suffolk County to prepare a preservation and use plan for its 1,157-acre Montauk County Park.

Last month, the county's Department of Parks, Recreation and Conservation issued a request for proposals for the restoration and rehabilitation of a complex of historic buildings in the park as a first step in the overall plan. Sealed bids are due by Sept. 10.

A key goal is to find a compatible use for the buildings. The plan, which will take 10 years to fully implement, also calls for improving public access to the park and furthering awareness of its historic and archeological features. Work on the buildings must be completed within a year of a contract signing.

The buildings include historic Third House, a sprawling two-story wood-frame structure dating in part to 1806, which served as a residence for Theodore Roosevelt in 1898 when he and his Rough Riders and other veterans of the Spanish-American War were quarantined at Camp Wikoff in Montauk.

The county's suggested uses for Third House, several cabins to the rear of it and the grounds around them include a bed and breakfast, a country inn, an educational/conference center, a dude ranch and a youth hostel. A successful bidder would complete the restoration, at an estimated cost of $500,000, at its own expense and operate the complex under a concession agreement with the county. Deep Hollow Ranch, a riding stable, is already in operation as a concession.

The proposal that a private entity rehabilitate the buildings for a profit-making operation has angered preservationists who consider such a move a crass commercial invasion of public lands.

Montauk County Park, one of the most magnificent in the bicounty park system, is also one of the least known and least utilized. Situated between Lake Montauk and a 724-acre state park, it is dotted with ponds and criss-crossed by trails that wind alternately through dense woods and swamp and then swing upland to open country with panoramic views. The park's beachfront stretches for three miles along Block Island Sound.

CITY STREETS/COUNTRY FUN:

The historic two-story Third House is one of the buildings proposed for renovation in Montauk County Park.

Suffolk County Division of Historic Services

"We're fighting to prevent this park from being privatized," said Rav Freidel, president of a local nonprofit group called Concerned Citizens for Montauk that was formed in 1970 to oppose development of the park.

"This park was acquired by the county in 1970 and paid for in 1970, and now because the county is in a financial crisis they are earmarking this park as a way to make money," he said. The county has extended the deadline for sealed bids from Aug. 26 to Sept. 10 to allow nonprofits to submit proposals.

To call this plan "privatization" is completely false, said Edward E. Wankel, Suffolk's Parks Commissioner.

"WE are trying to preserve this site in its historic context and we are looking for someone to manage this facility the way we would manage it," he said. "I will retain control of Third House, but the difference is that this person or persons will make the capital investment to make it work and we will share the profit."

The successful bidder will be expected to incorporate educational and interpretative programs with the commercial venture, and to keep an existing Indian museum an integral part of the site and possibly even expand it to a second building overlooking a former Indian village. Local groups that now occasionally use Third House for meetings must be allowed to continue doing so, Mr. Wankel said. Any default would result in a cancellation of the concession.

The proposal for the Third House complex is one of 21 similar initiatives to upgrade facilities in county parks at no cost while generating new income, Mr. Wankel said.

MONTAUK COUNTY PARK

The New York Times

The 21 projects are expected to earn the county $2 million a year and to bring in a capital investment of $29 million. The department's annual budget is currently about $8 million, of which 88 percent is covered by fees and other revenue.

The reality now is that in many instances bringing in a private investor "is the only way government, from the Federal level down, can maintain that which they have acquired," said Zachary N. Studenroth, the executive director of the Huntington Historical Society. His group undertook a study of the Third House site for the county and its potential for re-use and found that a hostelry was in keeping with what had historically occurred there.

The winning bidder would operate Third House for 10 years starting Jan. 1, 1993, with two 5-year options to renew the contract subject to the county's approval. The conces-

and $75,000 a year thereafter. In addition, the county would get a percentage of gross sales exceeding $500,000 annually.

Third House got its name because it was the third house built in Montauk for those tending cattle on 10,000 acres of common pasture. The original structure, built in 1747, was replaced by a new building in 1806. In the 1880's, the house was expanded to accommodate tourists as Montauk began developing into a resort community.

IN the late 1930's, the house and 33 surrounding acres were operated as the Deep Hollow Guest & Cattle Ranch, complete with restaurant and bar and accommodations for 30 guests. In the 1940's, nine cabins were built to house additional guests and later the addition of a four-unit motel and a swimming pool completed the transition to a modern resort.

"We're trying to restore an asset and bring it back to life," said J. Lance Mallamo, director of the Division of Historic Services for the parks department, referring to the building complex. The park, he said, is heavily underutilized and unknown to many.

But damage to the environment if more people come in is a very real concern, said Kevin McDonald, vice president of Group for the South Fork, a preservationist group. "It's a delicate balancing act between providing access so people can enjoy the features the park presents, without having so much access that the very things people come to see are destroyed," he said.

But Mr. Wankel, the Parks Commissioner, said that the public can be assured that the right thing will be done at Montauk. "It is the jewel in our parks system," he said. "What

Even after an area is "saved" there are always problems. Attempts to commercialize the County Park were ultimately defeated, "for now." *New York Times*, Sunday, August 16, 1992.

to be a push by some people to try to nick away at land, even land that's already been saved, and try to acquire it and establish it for their own. That's why it's so important to go to Town Board meetings.... So, I don't think it [the work] is ever going to end, as people will always be looking to make a buck.

"All along it's been an issue of not only obtaining the property, but also protecting it," says Richard Kahn. To underscore his view, he cites the problems with the Army Corps of Engineers in their unlimited digging for possible unexploded ordnance on the fragile bluffs of Camp Hero, "because the machines of the ACOE can't tell the difference between shrapnel and ferrous rock." On behalf of CCOM, Kahn sent a letter to Luz Span Labatto of the ACOE, recommending that they "not undertake any activities that may impact the fragile environment and bluff ecosystem." The letter expressed a need for regular inspection with removal of ordinance found on the beach. "CCOM recommends that ACOE use institutional controls (flyers, signs) to inform the public and visitors to Camp Hero of any possible risk," he wrote. That has come to pass.

Richard White, Jr. seems to corroborate this view. He believes that basically there is no more land to preserve, and therefore the pressing issue now is one of stewardship. "Be careful! Be very, very careful!" he admonishes. When asked to amplify the meaning of the warning, he says, "You've got all this open space and now you're going to have different people wanting different things, and the land is there, and if you're not careful..."

His concerns were echoed in CCOM's September 2003 newsletter. Captioned A LITTLE HISTORY, the article recalled that in 1924 the titles for Hither Hills State Park and Montauk Point State Park were taken by the Long Island State Parks Commission. Efforts to purchase the land had failed, and the Commission took the property by eminent domain to ensure that part of the Montauk Peninsula would be available to the public for park purposes. However, no park preserve status has been given as of yet to this property, leaving open the possibility for development of such active recreations as golf.

The issue of stewardship and the need for preservation status of the parkland near the point has arisen before. This was shown when commercialization was attempted at Theodore Roosevelt County Park and was successfully challenged. The recent history of Camp Hero, given to the state by the federal government to be used exclusively for passive recreation, provides another prime example of the problem. State Parks Commissioner Bernadette Castro has been consistent in her attempts to seek income-producing ideas—first a golf course, then cabins, and later a few token power windmills that would have been installed by LIPA (Long Island Power Authority). To date, all of these attempted incursions have been thwarted by CCOM's active vigilance.

Russell Stein also feels there is a misuse of public lands and that this may be the next major struggle. Stein sees reserved agricultural land further west, in East Hampton and beyond, being commercialized and turned into nurseries. He identifies the attempt to build a golf course at Camp Hero as another abuse. "Just because you have something that's public, doesn't mean your battle is over," he says. He expresses another concern:

> We saved half the land here, and that was a wonderful and necessary battle.... The half we didn't save is being brutalized in a way I never dreamed possible.... brutalized with houses larger than the motels we used to worry about. Now, at the height of the season, [these MacMansions] have 10 or 12 cars... in front of them. It's too late.... Pogo said, "We've met the enemy and he is us." What you have now is people driving 10-mile-a-gallon SUVs and clearing one-acre lawns [as opposed to retaining native vegetation]. I think you're going to find it hard to fight [that].

Stein recalls Montauk Moorland resident Carrie Nye telling the East Hampton Town ZBA about a new proposed eyesore. "For 100 years, people came to Montauk to hide. Now they come to show off." Stein concludes that "there's plenty for CCOM to do."

Current CCOM President Bill Akin conveys an optimistic view that the organization has helped educate and develop an environmental sense as to why Montauk is unique, and that there is "a good chance of keeping that going." But he also expresses concern about the increasing pressure for development. "The more we succeed in preserving things, the more unique we are, the more pressure, the higher the value [of Montauk] will be, the harder the fights will be." He expresses hope that the new Town comprehensive plan will result in some leveling off of the growth. "Whether that happens or not, what we've got to do is stay vigilant, keep people involved, get new members as we recently have, and get people on board who are willing to fight."

In writing in his newsletter column about the saving of Shadmoor at the end of the year 2000, Akin gave credit to many people and organizations—including the politicians—for doing the work to save that unique acreage:

But the greatest thanks must be directed to those who go unnoticed and in some instances almost forgotten. Those people who for no other reasons than a deep love for the land, made phone calls, wrote letters, took pictures (even made movies), showed up at meetings, and generally would only accept the word Saved, instead of Sold.

These concerned citizens are the very backbone of CCOM. They are those who could only answer affirmatively with their hearts, minds, energies, time, and talents to the pivotal question posed in 1970 and equally urgent in 2005: Do you love Montauk?

Glossary

Abbreviations of Agencies, Organizations, and Other Terms

AARP	American Association of Retired Persons
ACOE	Army Corps of Engineers
CAC	Citizens Advisory Committee
CCOM	Concerned Citizens of Montauk
COA	Clean Ocean Action
CPF	Community Preservation Fund
DEC	Department of Environmental Conservation
DEIS	Draft Environmental Impact Study
EIS	Environmental Impact Study
ELA	East Lake Association
EPA	Environmental Protection Agency
EQBA	Environmental Quality Bond Act
FLIS	Friends of Long Island Sound
GEIS	Generic Environmental Impact Statement
GSA	General Services Administration
GSF	Group for the South Fork ("The Group")
HUD	Housing and Urban Development
LILCO	Long Island Lighting Company

LIPA	Long Island Power Authority
MBCA	Marine Beach and Coastal Alliance
MBPOA	Montauk Beach Property Owners Association
MFCN	Marine Fish Conservation Network
MTA	Metropolitan Transit Authority
MVA	Montauk Village Association
NDZ	No Discharge Zone
NLT	National Land Trust
NMFS	National Marine Fisheries Service
NOAA	National Oceanographic and Atmospheric Administration
NPCA	National Parks Conservatory Agency
NRC	Nuclear Regulatory Commission
NRDC	Natural Resources Defense Council
NYS	New York State
OE	Unexploded Ordnance
PLT	Peconic Land Trust
SCWA	Suffolk County Water Authority
SEEDS	Sustainable East End Development Strategies
SEQRA	State Environmental Quality Review Act
SHAD	Shad Alliance
SOC	Shoreham Opponents Coalition
TNC	The Nature Conservancy
TPL	Trust for Public Land
TRA	Tuthill Road Association
ZBA	Zoning Board of Appeals

CCOM Presidents

Hilda Lindley   1970–1976

Tom Carley   1976–1978

Helen Sarvis   1978–1980
(appointed to Town Planning Board)

Dorothy Disken   1980–1982

Richard Johnson   1982–1983
(ran in Republican primary for Town Supervisor)

Carol Morrison   1983–1991

Rav Freidel   1992–1996

Lisa Grenci   1996–1997
(ran for Town Councilwoman)

Bill Akin   1997–present

Chronology: CCOM Issues by Year

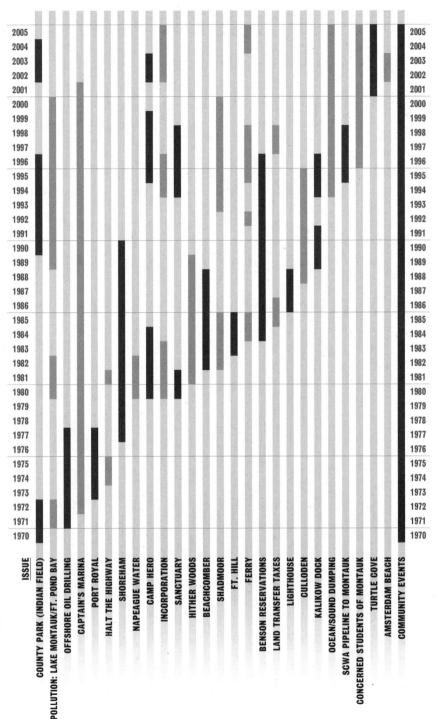

Map of Montauk

New York State Parks, County Preserves, and East Hampton Town Reserved Land

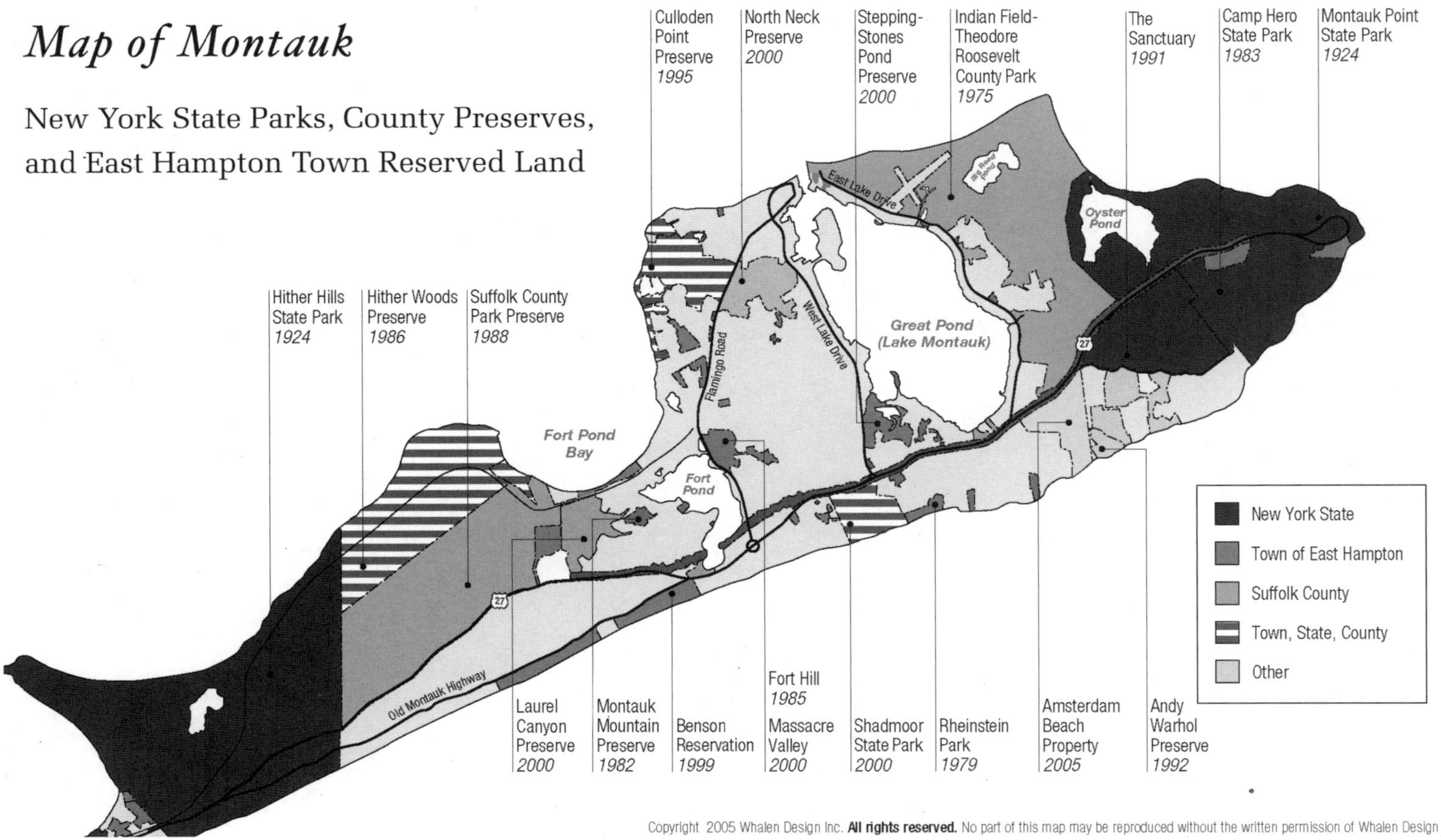

Legend:
- New York State
- Town of East Hampton
- Suffolk County
- Town, State, County
- Other

Labels (clockwise):

- Hither Hills State Park 1924
- Hither Woods Preserve 1986
- Suffolk County Park Preserve 1988
- Culloden Point Preserve 1995
- North Neck Preserve 2000
- Stepping-Stones Pond Preserve 2000
- Indian Field-Theodore Roosevelt County Park 1975
- The Sanctuary 1991
- Camp Hero State Park 1983
- Montauk Point State Park 1924
- Andy Warhol Preserve 1992
- Amsterdam Beach Property 2005
- Rheinstein Park 1979
- Shadmoor State Park 2000
- Massacre Valley 2000
- Fort Hill 1985
- Benson Reservation 1999
- Montauk Mountain Preserve 1982
- Laurel Canyon Preserve 2000

Map features:
- Oyster Pond
- Great Pond (Lake Montauk)
- East Lake Drive
- West Lake Drive
- Flamingo Road
- Fort Pond
- Fort Pond Bay
- Old Montauk Highway
- 27